CREATION,
EVOLUTION,
AND GOD'S WORD

CREATION, EVOLUTION, AND GOD'S WORD

Paul A. Zimmerman
Editor

Concordia Publishing House
St. Louis   London

Concordia Publishing House, St. Louis, Missouri
Concordia Publishing House, Ltd., London E.C. 1
Copyright © 1972 Concordia Publishing House
Library of Congress Catalog Card No. 70-182220
ISBN 0-570-03122-2

MANUFACTURED IN THE UNITED STATES OF AMERICA

Foreword

The essays contained in this book were originally delivered to various conferences of pastors and teachers of The Lutheran Church—Missouri Synod. In response to many requests for copies of the presentations they were then printed in limited edition under the title *Essays from the Creationist Viewpoint* (1966).

It is our hope that their publication in the present revised and updated form will make them available to a wider circle of readers. We believe that they present a critique of evolution and a defense of creationism that is both Biblical and scientific.

Ann Arbor, Mich.   PAUL A. ZIMMERMAN

Contents

Evolution: An Overview and Examination of Evidences

John W. Klotz, Ph. D.

Words have a habit of changing their meanings: the dictionary of one generation is rarely appropriate for the next. For that reason it is necessary to define the way in which terms are being used. This is especially true in the field of science. Copernicus would hardly recognize the theory that bears his name today: indeed it is a fair statement that no one today accepts the Copernican theory if we understand that term to mean the theory which Copernicus himself developed.

It is also true that Darwin would scarcely recognize the theory of evolution today. This is not to say that he would disagree with it; he simply would not recognize it. Indeed we rarely speak of Darwinism today; we usually use the term "neo-Darwinism," and by that we mean the general principles which Darwin developed as they have been modified and have sometimes been given entirely different meanings, as is the case with "fitness," which today is defined not in terms of individual survival but of reproductive effectiveness.

It is true that we must distinguish between neo-Darwinism and evolution: neo-Darwinism is only one of the theories of evolution. Yet neo-Darwinism is probably the most widely accepted present-day theory of evolution.

A great deal of confusion arises because the term "evolution" may be used in a variety of ways. It may be used as synonymous with development. Thus we may speak of the evolution of the motor car, the evolution of the modern newspaper, the evolution of our cities. Evolution may also be used as a synonym for change: we may speak of the evolution of cloud patterns.

But the scientific theory of evolution involves much more. To the biologist and to the scientist, evolution is the idea that the wide variety of living things can be explained by assuming that nonliving matter became alive, that from this single (or at most from a very few) instance(s) all the presently living organisms are descended, that man himself developed from animals that were not human, and that all of this took place through natural processes without any supernatural intervention.

When we say that we do not accept the theory of evolution, it is this idea—the origin of all living things ultimately from nonliving matter through purely natural processes—that we do not accept. We are not denying the fact of change. It is evident that the world today is quite different from that which first existed. It is evident that the landscape continues to change and also that living things change. It is evident that new species arise. But what we are saying is that we do not accept the idea of the origin of all living things from a single ancestor who in turn had originated from nonliving matter, and we do not accept the idea that all of this came about through purely natural processes.

Microevolution and Macroevolution

Some people find it helpful to distinguish between microevolution and macroevolution or between the general theory of evolution and the special theory of evolution. Microevolution includes all the changes that we are able to observe in living things, including the origin of new species. It is simply a recognition of the fact that all things change: this itself is a Biblical concept, Ps. 102:25-27, for only God is changeless.

It is macroevolution that refers to the generally held concept of evolution that we have outlined above. The special theory of evolution is in general synonymous with microevolution — the idea of change — and the general theory of evolution is usually equated with macroevolution. As we have indicated, no knowledgeable person questions microevolution or the special theory of evolution: the controversy comes when we discuss macroevolution and the general theory of evolution.

Thus the critical question is not whether change has taken place but rather whether change of the magnitude postulated by the theory of macroevolution has taken place. Bold says: "While there no longer can be doubt that living species are changing constantly, as evidenced by the recorded spontaneous and induced appearance of perceptible morphological and physiological mutations, the observation of such changes does not invalidate creationism with respect to ultimate origin." [1]

No Controlled Observation and Experimentation in Macroevolution

One of the problems of a study of evolution is the limited amount of controlled experimentation and observation that is possible. The genius of the scientific method is controlled experimentation, the technique whereby cause-and-effect relationships can be established with a reasonable degree of certainty. We do this by setting up a test and control which are as nearly identical as possible except with regard

11

to the factor we are testing. It is through this method that modern science has made its tremendous progress.

Experimentation is possible in the area of microevolution, and these are the experiments that are usually referred to as experimental confirmation of the theory of macroevolution. But they are not that. Any bearing these studies have on the problem of macroevolution consists of extrapolations from the data, and extrapolation is always hazardous. Mark Twain wrote:

> In the space of one hundred and seventy-six years the Lower Mississippi has shortened itself two hundred and forty-two miles. That is an average of a trifle over one mile and a third per year. Therefore, any calm person, who is not blind or idiotic, can see that in the Old Oölitic Silurian Period, just a million years ago next November, the Lower Mississippi River was upward of one million three hundred thousand miles long, and stuck out over the Gulf of Mexico like a fishingrod. And by the same token any person can see that seven hundred and forty-two years from now the Lower Mississippi will be only a mile and three-quarters long, and Cairo and New Orleans will have joined their streets together, and be plodding comfortably along under a single mayor and a mutual board of aldermen. There is something fascinating about science. One gets such wholesale returns of conjecture out of such a trifling investment of fact.[2]

The very nature of the problem makes it impossible to conduct experiments and observations related to macroevolution. It is simply not possible to carry out experiments that will demonstrate the amount of change required by the theory of macroevolution.

Stebbins recognizes this when he says:

To be sure no biologist has actually seen the origin by evolution of a major group of organisms. Nevertheless races and species have been produced by duplicating in the laboratory and gardens some of the evolutionary processes known to take place in nature. The reason that major steps in evolution have never been observed is that they require millions of years to be completed. The evolutionary processes which gave rise to major groups of organisms, such as genera and families, took place in the remote past, long before there were people to observe them. Nevertheless, the facts which we know about these origins . . . provide very strong circumstantial evidence to indicate that the processes which brought them about were very similar to those found in modern groups of animals and plants which are evolving all around us today.[3]

Dobzhansky says: "Anti-evolutionists have said again and again that evolution is not 'proven.' We cannot reproduce in the laboratory the changes which transformed the three-toed horse into the one-toed one or those which led *Australopithecus* to *Homo*. It is an inference (and at that one questioned by some competent authorities) that the bones of our ancestors were once upon a time not very different from those of *Australopithecus*. Darwin did not claim to have observed evolution except that under domestication. He claimed that evolution can be inferred from what he did observe."[4]

Rostand observes: "The three cardinal problems of biology—the problem of how a living creature grows, the problem of how species evolve, the problem of how life originated—have scarcely been touched by scientists . . . we have hardly any idea of the way in which the organic metamorphoses that must have gone to produce the human species from some original virus may have been accomplished in the course of ages." [5]

Wallace remarks:

> Any person who is firmly and unalterably convinced that each of today's species of plants and animals arose by an act of special creation will find no evidence . . . that will compel him to change his mind. There simply is no such evidence, nor can there ever be. A Divine Being of infinite wisdom . . . could have created living forms in a manner that would have dribbled off as by-products all of these things we have gleaned as evidence for evolution. We can only say that He went about His task in a way that mimicked evolution in every detail; it is unfortunate that some event did not occur which would have clearly ruled out evolutionary theory.[6]

Wallace is repeating the old cliché that those who reject the theory of evolution still believe today that God created every species in its present form. Aside from that, the last part of his statement is interesting. He assumes that if evolution has not occurred, God deceives by giving the impression that it has occurred or at least is playing cat-and-mouse games with men. There is, however, another alternative, and that is that the majority of even the most capable human beings do not yet have the evidence or are not intelligent enough to interpret the evidence. For 2,000 years the most intelligent scientists thought the solar system was geocentric even though a heliocentric system was suggested already by Aristarchus of Samos in the third century B. C. It was not that God deceived in creating a solar system that appeared geocentric; it was that men did not have all the evidence and were not intelligent enough to properly interpret the evidence they had.

Thus acceptance of the theory of evolution is in a very real sense a matter of faith. Bruce Stewart in discussing the teaching of evolution quotes Conant's discussion of the scientific method: "Take up a textbook of these subjects and see how very simple it all seems as far as method is concerned and how very complicated the body of facts and principles soon becomes. Indeed before you have got far in a freshman course you will find the harassed professor under pressure to be up to date in bringing in subjects which cannot be adequately analyzed by the class. Having insufficient knowledge of other disciplines . . . the students have to take on faith statements about scientific laws and the structure of matter which are almost as dogmatic as though they were handed down by a high priest." [7]

The Origin of Life

One reason why controlled experimentation is not possible is that it is impossible to determine and to duplicate the environmental conditions of the past. Thus Harold Urey has suggested that the earth's original atmosphere was a mixture of methane, hydrogen, ammonia, and water vapor. Combining these into amino acids, the building blocks of the proteins, would require a substantial amount of energy, and Urey believes this came from cosmic rays, only a few of which penetrate the earth at present because of the presence of ozone in the upper atmosphere. At his suggestion S. L. Miller exposed a mixture of these gases to a continuous electric discharge in 1953 and found that some amino acids were produced. Amino acids combine in a process of polymerization which involves the loss of water molecules. Ordinarily polymerization can be accomplished only at relatively high temperatures; however, S. W. Fox discovered that in the presence of phosphoric acid this reaction would occur at temperatures as low as 70°C. He also reported that when one mixes together 18 amino acids common to living systems, these are not distributed in a haphazard fashion but exhibit a considerable number of nonrandom combinations. Using energy from the sun and from cosmic rays, organic molecules are thus believed to have accumulated in the seas. These formed primitive living things which began to metabolize in a fermentation process; this released carbon dioxide into the primitive atmosphere, and other anaerobic processes followed.

Later photophosphorylation processes came into use. These use the energy of light to provide high-energy organic phosphates. Photophosphorylation was followed by photosynthesis; this released oxygen as a byproduct. Some of this oxygen was changed into ozone, which today serves to screen out most of the cosmic rays. The absence of oxygen prior to this time prevented the oxidation of the relatively simple compounds which could exist in a reducing atmosphere but would have been destroyed in the present oxidizing atmosphere. Thus it is suggested that life originated under circumstances quite different from those found on earth today, that life changed the environment in such a way that nonliving material can no longer become alive.

There are many problems to this theory. There is the problem of free energy mobilization, and there is the problem of the origin of protein. There is also a problem with the origin of chlorophyll and photosynthesis.

Moreover, we should point out that there is no evidence that the conditions postulated by these researchers actually existed on earth. What we do know is that nonliving matter is not becoming alive today; the careful work of Louis Pasteur demonstrated this. It takes a great deal of faith to believe that chance could bring about changes such as these.

Complexities

It also takes a great deal of faith to believe that chance

could develop the complexities we see in the universe about us. Photosynthesis itself is a very complex process. Steward says that every high school student now professes to know how protein is made because he has learned this in high school and in popular magazines, but he asks whether a company set up to make protein in a protein-poor world, on whose board of directors all the recent Nobel Prize winners might serve, would succeed. He answers: "Perhaps in another century, but not in this decade." He also says: "Despite the most glowing scientific brochures, I would not buy shares in a company floated to do this." Living cells, he points out, have intrinsic properties by virtue of their organization, the subtle way in which they are put together that enables them to do these things. Cells take the biochemically and biophysically feasible events which can be demonstrated *in vitro* to an often high degree, and by a subtle sort of biological engineering they render the merely feasible to be practical.[8]

How complicated this process is is evident from the research of Ake Gustafsson of Sweden, who estimates that from 250 to 300 gene loci in barley are concerned with the synthesis of chloroplasts, so that the synthesis of only one component of the process is itself extremely complex. Chloroplast development consists of a large sequence of gene control processes which must be coordinated so as to follow each other in a precisely integrated fashion. (Stebbins, pp. 32 f.)

Another scientist says that after a lifetime of studying living things he has become a vitalist because he is convinced that living things obey physicochemical laws but apply these laws on an essentially new plane. He says he cannot share the confidence expressed at the Moscow Symposium in 1957 as to the possibility of creating living systems out of inanimate matter.[9] He finds it difficult to believe that the living cell is only a pot full of enzymes.

17

Still another scientist is quoted as saying that in the light of our present knowledge of physics and chemistry we cannot understand the transition from chemical to life.[10]

E. N. Willmer writes:

> The internal organization of the cell is unbelievably complex on the molecular and even submicroscopic level. The result therefore obtained by making extracts of cells or tissues is not unlike trying to find out the plan of the practical course in biological chemistry at a university by applying the most modern and efficient demolition machinery (cf. the Waring blender) to the biochemical laboratory, with all its contained and systematically arranged chemicals, and then analyzing the fluid that subsequently runs down the drains. The main differences between the two situations would seem to be that the biological materials are much less reactive and the enzymes in general very much more specific in their actions than most of the reagents in the chemical laboratory. The organization of the reactions has, however, been broken down in both cases.[11]

The Fitness of the Environment

It is also difficult to believe that by chance the earth happens to have the right environment for life as we know it. The earth is placed just the proper distance from the sun. Life can exist for any length of time only between 0°C. and 100°C., the freezing and boiling points of water respectively. Actually the practical limits are even narrower because of the susceptibility of proteins and enzymes — so essential to living things and life processes — to even moderately high temperatures: most proteins and enzymes break down if they are subjected to temperatures in excess of 40°C. for any length of time, so that most organisms live between 0°C. and 40°C. If the earth were closer to the sun, the temperature would be higher, and life would be impossible. If we were farther from the sun, temperatures would be lower, and once more life would be impossible. Moreover, it is important that the earth should revolve on its axis. If the earth always presented the same face to the sun, as the moon always presents the same face to the earth, one hemisphere would be relatively hot, the other relatively cold.

The sun itself is a star of the right size: a larger star would generate too much heat and exert too much gravitational attraction.

Three minor constituents of our atmosphere — water vapor, carbon dioxide, and ozone — also contribute to climatic conditions here on earth. These minor gases screen us from the action of the sun's ultraviolent rays. On the daylight side of the earth they shield us from the heat of the infrared solar rays, and on the nighttime side they blanket the surface from the cosmic cold of space. Without these minor constituents, which make up less than 2% of the volume of the earth's atmosphere, the earth would be intolerably warm on the daylight side and inhospitably cold on the nighttime side.

Water, an Unusual Substance

Water itself is an unusual substance. Its high specific heat, its high heat of fusion, its high heat of vaporization, the fact that it reaches its greatest density at 4°C., the greenhouse effect of water vapor, the fact that water is as close to a universal solvent as any substance — all make it difficult to believe that this very common substance just happened to have properties so essential to living things. It is evident, then, that it requires even more faith to believe in chance than it does to believe in creation through an all-wise and all-powerful God.

You take your choice: You worship either the god of chance or the God of the Bible.

Caution Advised

Ehrlich and Holm plead for what they call a "non-Euclidean" theory of evolution: they themselves accept evolution but do not want to be placed in the position of having to affirm a "belief" in evolution. They feel that the current theories are extremely dogmatic and say: "The most obvious aspect of evolutionary theory that may be at least partially explained as a reaction to the Bishop Wilberforce approach has been the development of a rather stringent orthodoxy. This orthodoxy is easily detected in the compulsion of biologists to affirm *belief* in evolution (rather than to accept it as a highly satisfactory theory) and to list *proofs* that evolution has occurred. . . . The discipline is . . . close enough to the danger area to call for some critical reexamination of its basic tenets."

They believe that the strong urge to believe in the present evolutionary theory stems partly from the very common human error that one of a number of current explanations *must* be correct, and they say that demonstrating special creation to be scientifically meaningless (and it is obviously scientifically meaningless, since science excludes consideration of the supernatural) does not "prove" that the theory of evolution is correct. They believe that current faith in the theory is reminiscent of many other ideas which at one time were thought to be self-evidently true and supported by all available data—the flat earth, the geocentric universe, the sum of the angles of a triangle equaling 180°.[12]

Hanson also calls attention to the danger of assuming that facts can be interpreted in only one way. He says:

> Facts are always facts about, or with respect to, or set out in terms of some theoretical framework. Should the framework deliquesce, the objects, processes, and

facts will dissolve conceptually. Where are now the "facts" of alchemy, of the phlogiston theory? Or must we grant that no observations ever really supported such frameworks of ideas? Where can one now locate a sample of caloric, or a magnetic effluvium? How easy and doctrinaire to mark these as chimerae, as illusions of fact. They are actually once-descriptive references whose supporting rationale has disappeared. Their articulators were, in their way, dedicated empiricists, groping, struggling to delineate *the facts* concerning intricacies of a nearly incomprehensible world. But effluvia, caloric, phlogiston, influences, virtues, humors, essences, harmonies, attractions, and powers—these are no longer sustained by laws as once they appeared to be and as *our* now recorded facts, processes, and objects seem so surely to be. But the negative-energy electron of 1928, the luminiferous ether, and the planet Vulcan of the 19th century are not so long departed from the scientific stage. May not the solid acquisitions of our own laboratory performances yet grow pale before the chilling winds of new doctrine—doctrine opposed to our presently accepted theories? [13]

Uniformity and Uniformitarianism

In science one deals not only with facts but also with assumptions. These latter by their very nature cannot be demonstrated; they must be taken for granted. The assumptions of the evolutionist also have a bearing on the theory. One assumption of the scientist is that of unformity: that scientific principles and laws hold throughout time and space. We assume that nature is regular rather than capricious. We assume that gravity is universal and that matter behaves in the same way in the vast reaches of space as it behaves on earth.

We further assume that gravity has always acted as it does today and that matter has always behaved as it behaves today.

This principle is thoroughly Biblical, for the God whom we worship, the God of the Bible, is a God of order. Moreover, it is only by assuming uniformity that science is possible and that the pursuit of the scientific enterprise is worthwhile. If nature were capricious, if prediction were not possible, there would be little incentive and motivation for scientific research. For this reason the principle of uniformity, though it is an assumption, is generally accepted.

Associated with the principle of uniformity is the principle of uniformitarianism. This assumes a uniformity of rates: that natural processes have always gone on at the same rate at which they are going on at present — "The present is the key to the past." Uniformitarianism has been especially important in geology, where until very recently it was regarded as having settled the controversy between the catastrophists and the uniformitarians. The catastrophists suggested that the strata with their different plants and animals could be understood on the basis of a series of catastrophes which wiped out the plant and animal life of one period and that in the next the particular area was populated with plants and animals which came in from a remote area unaffected by the catastrophe and that these too were subsequently wiped out by a catastrophe.

The uniformitarians sought an explanation for the changing plants and animals of the different strata in the gradual changes taking place in organisms so that the large changes represented in the different geological strata were regarded as evidences for macroevolution.

In the last few years uniformitarianism has come to be questioned. A recent president of the American Geological Society is quoted as saying: "Geology suffers from a great lack of data and in such a situation any attractive theory that comes along is taken as gospel. That is the case with uniformitarianism. Geology students are taught that 'the present is the key to the past,' and they too often take it to mean that nothing ever happened that isn't happening now. But since the end of World War II, when a new generation moved in, we have gathered more data, and we have begun to realize that there were many catastrophic events in the past, some of which happened just once." He himself, he tells us, is in favor of junking both terms — catastrophism and uniformitarianism — because they are "just too confusing." [14]

We have been able to observe many developments that took place more rapidly than was once thought possible. The volcano Paricutin in Mexico erupted in 1943, continued erupting until 1952, and built up a cone over 1,500 feet in height. Similarly a new island, Surtsey, appeared as a result of volcanic activity off the south coast of Iceland in 1963. What is particularly interesting is the rapidity with which this new island was colonized by plant life and animal life even though the climate is relatively cold.[15]

Other processes, too, may go on faster than might seem possible. In commenting on the rate of shore erosion at Woods Hole, Massachusetts, Jack Hough says: "The question will be raised . . . of how much time is required for the development of shore features of this magnitude. Observations bearing on this question were made in an area near Woods Hole, Massachusetts, after the hurricane of 1938. The amount of shore erosion which occurred during the hurricane in a period of a few hours exceeded that which had occurred during the previous fifty years. The geological doctrine of uniformitarianism, stressing the slow orderly working of familiar processes, has perhaps blinded us to the importance of the unusual and catastrophic event." [16]

The Effect of the Theory on Biology

Studies of evolution stimulated by the publication of

Darwin's *Origin* have resulted in narrow specialization and in laboratory research as opposed to field observations. This is indeed ironic because Darwin himself was a naturalist and devoted his life to field observations. Yet the result of his theory was to drive scientists into the laboratory. Moreover, specialization such as followed the development of the theory is likely to lead to a failure to synthesize. The laboratory researcher is likely to miss the forest because he is concerned with the trees.

One of the reasons for our present environmental crisis is the overemphasis on specialization, on laboratory research, and on one-problem solutions. Particular problems have indeed been solved, but at times this has been done at the expense of creating other problems.

The theory of evolution with its doctrine of progress has also encouraged exploitation of natural resources. It has inculcated the idea of man's superiority over animals and has done this much more effectively than the much-faulted Genesis account; it has suggested that if they cannot survive in competition with man, then they may properly be eliminated; this is the way in which natural selection works, for nature is "red in tooth and claw." The doctrine of progress and the doctrine of natural selection have led some men to a ruthless extermination of species which supposedly are not able to compete.

Elder in his *Crisis in Eden* points this out. He favors the approach of some evolutionists such as Loren Eiseley but remarks that others such as Pierre Teilhard have encouraged the idea that man is separate (and superior) to nature. He calls such individuals "exclusionists" and believes that their point of view has contributed to our environmental crisis.[17]

Evidences for Evolution

What about the evidences for evolution? We can divide

these into three general categories. First of all there are evidences of similarity which are believed to point to a common ancestor. Then there is the evidence of the fossil record, which is supposed to indicate that changes of the magnitude postulated by macroevolution have taken place. Finally there are a variety of mechanisms suggested whereby evolution may have occurred.

Similarities

To attempt to examine all the evidence for evolution from similarity of structure, physiological function, biochemical makeup, embryology, and the like would require more space than we have available in this brief treatment. It might be helpful, however, to examine the underlying assumptions in the various arguments that are presented from similarity and to examine a few of these arguments.

The basic assumption is that similarity is evidence of descent from a common ancestor. It is believed that the greater the resemblance the closer the common ancestor. For this reason all sorts of similarities are sought between man and the anthropoids, because the anthropoids are believed to be the closest of man's common ancestors.

This argument that similarity is evidence of descent from a common ancestor really represents a shift in logic. It is true, of course, that individuals descended from a common ancestor tend to resemble one another, but it is not true that individuals who resemble one another are necessarily closely related and inherit those similarities from a common ancestor. Thus all members of the cat family have long canine teeth, but this does not mean that any animal with long canine teeth is a member of the cat family.

It is a well-known fact that human beings may resemble one another very closely and not be closely related. We all have our "twins" whom we may not know and whom we in most cases never even meet.

Parallel Mutations

The fact of the matter is that we have experimental evidence that at least some resemblances have not been inherited from a common ancestor. Similar mutations may occur in different species. *Drosophila melanogaster* and *D. simulans* are separate species. Both have experienced mutations of eye color to prune, ruby, and garnet; of body color to yellow; of bristle shapes to forked; and of wings to crossveinless, vesiculated, and rudimentary. Thus a *D. melanogaster* and a *D. simulans* may both have a ruby eye. Yet we know they have not inherited that ruby eye from a common ancestor but rather from two separate ancestors, for the same type of mutation has occurred in both species.

Some evolutionists have argued that parallel mutations are themselves evidence for evolution. They argue that the parallel mutation is possible only because the organisms are closely related and have the same sort of germ plasm. Yet we know of instances where parallel mutations or parallel variations cannot be due to the possession of a common ancestral germ plasm. Dobzhansky says: "Here is a caveat—phenotypically similar or mimetic mutants are produced also at different, fully complementary and not even linked genes within a species. . . . A few of these mimetic genes may conceivably have arisen in evolution through reduplication of the same ancestral genes. But for a majority such a supposition is quite gratuitous. Our powers of observation are limited, and what to our eyes are phenotypically similar changes may actually be due to different genes." [18]

Rensch points out that similar or identical organs may arise from quite different anatomical substrata. He calls our attention to the vasa malpighii, which originate from the ectoderm in insects and from the endoderm in spiders; and the stridulating ridges and spines of insects, which may develop on various parts of the legs, wings, thorax, or abdomen.[19]

Merrell says much the same: "Unfortunately not all similarities between members of different species are due to a common ancestry, and the concept has sometimes been considerably overworked. Lamarck and especially St. Hilaire argued that all animal species conformed to a common archetype, a clearly erroneous idea that was strongly and effectively attacked by Cuvier." [20]

It is also evident that the evolutionist chooses his resemblances. If they fit with what he believes to be the course of evolutionary development, they are cited as evidence for descent from a common ancestor. But if they do not fit with his elaborately constructed phylogenetic trees, they are regarded as instances of convergent evolution, cases in which under similar environmental conditions organisms develop similar structures even though they have not descended from a common ancestor. Thus the platypus, one of the strange mammals of Australia, is not regarded as a link between the birds and mammals even though it has a bill, webbed feet, and tarsal spurs.

In commenting on the relationship between man and the gorilla, Simpson says: "Zuckerkandl has shown 'from the point of view of hemoglobin structure, it appears that the gorilla is just an abnormal human, or man an abnormal gorilla, and the two species form actually one continuous population.' From any point of view other than that properly specified, that is of course nonsense. What the comparison seems really to indicate is that in this case at least hemoglobin is a bad choice and has nothing to tell us about affinities or indeed tells us a lie." He goes on to say that it does show that men and gorillas are rather closely related, but he believes that this fact has been known for a long time from the traditional morphological comparisons.[21]

Evidences from Embryology

Sometimes careful studies of the particular evidence for evolution show that the evidence is not so overwhelming as was once supposed or that it is no evidence at all. Much has been made of the embryological resemblances of different organisms. This particular line of evidence was developed by Ernst Haeckel, who suggested the biogenetic law: "Ontogeny recapitulates phylogeny." He meant to say that in the course of embryonic development (ontogeny) the organism repeats the evolutionary history of the phylum (phylogeny). And he and his successors traced out this development in a number of systems and organs.

Today this theory is not nearly so important in knowledgeable circles as popularizations of evolution would indicate. Ehrlich and Holm refer to it as a "crude interpretation of embryologic sequences," and they say it will not stand up on close examination. Its shortcomings have been almost universally pointed out by modern authors, they say, and they believe that the resemblances of early vertebrate embryos is readily explained without resort to mysterious forces "compelling each individual to reclimb its phylogenetic tree." [22]

Recent studies have indicated that the development often proceeds under the guidance of organizers which induce a differentiation of particular qualities out of the reacting tissues. Thus certain cells die and disappear not because they represent an ancestral stage but because they are needed at a certain stage as scaffolding or because they are actually needed during embryonic and larval life. Saunders, while expressing the opinion that in some cases the death and disappearance of cells has as its purpose the elimination of phylogenetic vestiges, believes that in other cases it is the usual method of eliminating organs and tissues useful only during embryonic or larval life. He says: "The principle conclusion to be drawn . . . is that the death of cells and the destruction of tissues, organs, and organ systems are programmed as normal morphogenetic events in the development of morphocellular organisms. . . . The present exploration has revealed that death during embryogenesis serves utilitarian goals in some instances at least, that its occurrence is subject to control by factors of the immediate cellular and humoral environment, and that aberrations in its normal pattern of expression provide the mechanism for the realization of many mutant phenotypes." [23]

Vestigial Organs

At one time the existence of the so-called vestigial organs was cited as an example of evolution. These are organs which at one time were thought to have had a function but supposedly lost it in the course of evolution and development. A number of organs are listed in this category: the appendix, the coccyx, the tonsils, the ear muscles, and the like.

Yet the fact that we are unable to assign a function to an organ is no evidence that it has none. For many years the role of the thymus was unknown. Because it is relatively small in the adult, it was thought to be functionless. Today we know that it is extremely important in immunological responses and plays a significant role in fetal and neonatal life. The cells that make it up form extremely rapidly during these periods. They are discharged into the circulating blood in large numbers shortly after birth and lodge in the lymph nodes, spleen, bone marrow, and other antibody-producing tissues. Here they become reticulum cells, and these in turn are activated by an invading organism and become converted into plasma cells. The plasma cells subsequently produce the antibodies. For this reason this organ, once thought to be

29

functionless, is known to have a very important function in protecting the body against the invasion of microorganisms.

Fossils

What about the fossil record? Today this is one of the chief lines of supporting evidence for the idea of macroevolution. There is no doubt that fossils are quite abundant and that most of them are quite different from the plants and animals we know today. The latter fact is interpreted by the evolutionist as evidence that change of a considerable magnitude has taken place.

We must remember, however, that we are dealing with the parts of the organisms that present the greatest classification problems. In plants we classify chiefly on the basis of flowers, but these are very rare among plant fossils. Rather we have the bark, bit of leaves, and the like, and we must seek to classify on this basis.

In animals we again have the hard parts: usually parts of the bony system and the teeth. These too create real classification problems. Of all systems the skeletal system is probably the most likely to be modified by environmental conditions which have no permanent hereditary effect and which therefore can have no evolutionary significance. Dietary deficiencies may alter the skeleton: rickets, for instance, results in marked skeletal changes. Endocrine disorders may also have a marked effect on the skeleton: an overactive pituitary may result in a pituitary giant, or if it becomes overactive after the individual has reached maturity, it will result in acromegaly. Disease may also alter the skeletal system: bovine tuberculosis in man may result in a hunchback. Although we must assume that the fossil we have is typical of the organism, there is always the annoying possibility that it may be atypical and may be the result of one of these disorders.

Not a Random Sample

Moreover, the fossil record is both an incomplete and a nonrandom sample. It is obvious, of course, that we do not have all forms preserved as fossils. But it is more significant that the sample is not a random sample. Ehrlich and Holm point out that fossils must be viewed as a very biased sample of the remains of past life (though they believe that the record is ample so that we may recognize many patterns).[24]

Davis believes that the paleontologist has the threads of a cross-section disconnected and fragmented because of deficiences in the record and further believes that his study is limited because it is restricted to a single system — the skeletal. These deficiencies, inherent in the record, he believes present a real problem to the evolutionist.[25]

The fact is that most fossils come from the shallow seas and lowland areas, where the chances of quick burial are greatest. Although we have a fairly complete record of the plant and animal life in these areas in the different geological periods, we do not know very much about plant and animal life in the prairies, the mountains, and other areas.

While Stebbins (pp. 134 f.) believes that the paleontologists have been able to supply us with a great deal of information regarding the course of evolution, he points out that the bias inherent in the fossil record is exactly of the wrong kind for evolutionists who wish to learn how the major groups of organisms originated. In modern plants and animals the greatest diversity of races and species exists in mountainous habitats, where climate, soil, and other factors can vary greatly in a small area. Moreover, in such regions new habitats are opened up much more often than in the flat lowlands. But these are the places in which the chances that fossils will be preserved are the lowest.

Human Evolution

In connection with the fossil record it is particularly interesting that the record of human evolution is quite meager and that recent studies of the human and prehuman remains have indicated that these forms are not nearly so different from modern man as was once supposed. Exotic names such as *Pithecanthropus erectus* and *Sinanthropus pekinensis* have been replaced by the name *Homo erectus*. It is generally agreed that the Neanderthal man should be classified as *Homo sapiens,* the species to which modern man is said to belong. An excellent detailed study of human fossils may be found in the recently published *Rock Strata and the Bible Record,* edited by Paul A. Zimmerman.[26]

The Mechanism

What about the mechanism for evolution, the means by which the changes on which natural selection depends are supposed to come about? It is in this area that modern genetics has made its greatest contribution. Although some believe that evolution has occurred in big jumps, it is generally agreed that more commonly evolution has occurred through the accumulation of small changes. These changes are believed to have been brought about largely by mutations.

Mutations

Mutations occur on an average of somewhere between 1 in 100,000 and 1 in 1,000,000. They are known in all organisms from bacteria to man. It is believed that they occur when the DNA code specifies an amino acid different from the one normally specified. Thus individuals suffering from sickle-cell anemia have hemoglobin that differs from normal hemoglobin in only one respect. It contains a unit of valine in the place of a unit of glutamic acid. The RNA "code" for valine is GUG (guanine, uracil, guanine), for glutamic acid GAG (guanine, adenine, guanine). Thus it may be that the production of sickle-cell hemoglobin arose from a change in which adenine (the "A" of the codon) was replaced by uracil (the "U" of the codon).

Most mutations are either lethal, semilethal, or subvital: they affect the reproductive rate adversely. Some of them kill the organism outright; others reduce its reproductive rate below those of the type individual. Most of them are harmful to the organism in some way: hemophilia, sickle-cell anemia, cystic fibrosis, and albinism, all of which are believed to be brought about by mutations in man, are examples of this. Mutations tend to recur: most of them appear several times in a period of years.

That they tend to reappear is favorable for evolution: this will tend to increase the frequency of mutation in the stock. However, it is hard to believe that a mechanism that is harmful and is likely to reduce the reproductive rate is a means for bringing about the changes required by the theory of evolution.

Evolutionists recognize that most mutations are harmful, but they argue that evolution is able to work with the few mutations that are favorable. Yet it is difficult to point to a mutation that is actually favorable. Most of them are pleiotropic: that is, they have a number of effects. One of these may be favorable, but others may be harmful, and the net effect may be harmful.

Increasing Mutant Frequency

Even if a mutation is favorable, it would take a long time for it to become established in the stock. Carter believes that a recessive gene with a selective advantage of 0.1%

would increase in frequency in a population from 0.001% to 1% in 309,780 generations and that it would go from 1% to 50% in 11,624 generations.[27] It is believed that the fact that mutations tend to recur will decrease the time required.

Preadaptation

It has also been suggested that organisms may be developing mutations which will be of use under future environmental conditions: preadaptation. Thus mutations supply a great deal of variety with which natural selection works not today but at some future period in the earth's history. It is suggested that the trait best adapted to some future environmental condition is recessive and less desirable in the present environment. The organism is protected against the undesirable effects of the recessive because it is covered by the dominant; yet it is also available for the changed future environment.

Yet natural selection must work now and with the materials at hand. It is hard to believe that selection would not act against neutral or harmful mutations to eliminate them before the environmental changes favorable to them appear.

That mutation is an adequate mechanism for the kinds of change and the extent of change needed by the theory of evolution is doubtful. Carson says that one of the great dilemmas in modern evolutionary theory is that most of the mutations found repeatedly in the forms that have been studied do not constitute the kind of differences that distinguish species.[28]

Medawar says that the main weakness of modern evolutionary theory is its lack of a fully worked out theory of variation. He says we have no convincing account of evolutionary progress, that is, of the inexplicable tendency of organisms to adopt ever more complicated solutions of the problems of remaining alive.[29]

34

In Summary

Thus we shall have to recognize that there are still many problems with the theory of evolution. There are evidences that change of a considerable magnitude has taken place. But things are not always what they seem to be: looking at facts from a different point of view often suggests an entirely different theory. For centuries observations of the heavenly bodies suggested a geocentric theory: the best scientists of the day accepted the idea that the earth was the center of the solar system and rejected the idea which had already been suggested centuries before Christ that the sun was the center of the solar system. Because evolution cannot be subjected to the technique of experimentation, it is very difficult to settle many of the questions that arise. Certainly as a minimum we will want to say: "Not proved." Certainly we would agree that the evidence we have would not support rejection of the creation account in Scripture.

Analysis of So-Called Evidences of Evolution

Wilbert H. Rusch Sr., M. S., Sc. S.

Contrary to the opinion of many, the debate concerning origins is not over. "Creation or Evolution" is still the subject of much controversy — both remaining the only viable theories of origins. A third theory, although much hoped for by many scientists, has still to appear on the scene.

To begin with, a delineation of the two theories is in order. The theory of creation holds that —

    a. God by His almighty word called matter into being, established natural laws, and created the basic "kinds" of plants and animals as well as man;

    b. all organisms now living have descended from organisms of the same created "kind";

    c. within these created "kinds" processes of change have occurred to produce individuals differing in various degrees from their ancestors, yet never sufficiently different to produce a new "kind" (e.g., the various breeds of dogs, the several races of man, both past and present); and

    d. such physical changes in organisms since their creation have arisen through degeneration that was due to the fall of man or through natural causes that are continuing in operation and therefore may be studied experimentally.

It is assumed that Christians would accept creation, yet on the basis of the Pentateuch of the Orthodox Jew and the Koran of the faithful Mohammedan these groups also number creationists in their ranks.

In the writer's opinion the theory of evolution is not as definitive as that of creation. This is borne out by the fact that Kerkut recognizes two usages of the term evolution. Kerkut (and Standen before him) underlines this when he concludes his *Implications* as follows: "There is a theory which states that many living animals can be observed over the course of time to undergo changes so that new species are formed. This can be called the 'Special Theory of Evolution' and can be demonstrated in certain cases by experiments." He goes on to say: "On the other hand, there is the theory that all living forms in the world have arisen from a single source which itself came from an inorganic form. This theory can be called the 'General Theory of Evolution,' and the evidence that supports it is not sufficiently strong to allow me to consider it as anything more than a working hypothesis." [1]

If the "Special Theory of Evolution" were all that was embodied in the concept of evolution, there would be little disagreement for many, since evolution as understood in Kerkut's "Special Theory" would be "variation with limits" to many creationists. However, the "General Theory of Evolution," also known as "amoeba to man" evolution, is the definition of evolution as used in the majority of science books written for the upper elementary, secondary, and undergraduate levels. It is this meaning of evolution that is used in this paper.

Now if it happens that more hold to one particular

philosophy than to a second, this does not make the first philosophy true. Truth is never determined by majority vote, and it could actually be that the minority view is the true one, the majority view being false. This can be applied to evolution: the number of people who believe in it is no guarantee of its truth. An honest person will accept factual things as real. On this there is no disagreement. However, the hypotheses drawn from such facts, as well as the hypothetical reconstruction of past events based on them, are all legitimate areas for differences. William H. George realized this when he wrote: "Facts remain but theories crumble." [2] James Conant underlined this when he said: "Statements about the past, predictions about the future, generalizations about what event will follow another, are all grist for the mill of the thoroughgoing sceptic." [3]

We find ourselves in a dilemma because those who subscribe to evolution will take a body of facts and interpret them one way, while those who subscribe to creation will take the same body of facts and interpret them another way. Actually neither interpretation can be proved; either must be accepted on faith. Kerkut points out that evolution is not a fact but is a working hypothesis (p. 157). Therefore the person who holds to evolution as a fact is really accepting it on faith.

The French biologist Louis Bounoure quoted Yves Delage, a late Sorbonne professor of zoology, as saying: "I readily admit that no species has ever been known to engender another, and that there is no absolutely definite evidence that such a thing has ever taken place. Nonetheless, I believe evolution to be just as certain as if it had been objectively proved." Bounoure adds the comment: "In short what science asks of us here is an act of faith, and it is in fact under the guise of a sort of revealed truth that the idea of evolution is generally put forward." [4] Bounoure, formerly president of the

Biological Society of Strasbourg, as well as director of the Zoological Museum and later director of research at the National Center of Scientific Research in France, also wrote: "Evolutionism is a fairy tale for grown-ups. This theory has helped nothing in the progress of science. It is useless" (ibid.). In a later article on the same subject, Bounoure supported this position by a quotation by a professor of paleontology at the Sorbonne, Jean Piveteau, who said that the science of facts as regards evolution "cannot accept any of the different theories which seek to explain evolution. It even finds itself in opposition with each one of these theories. There is something here which is both disappointing and disquieting." [5]

The plaintive cry is often heard that a person should not use an evolutionist's statement as a support for a creationist's point of view. However, if the evolutionist mentions a point that the creationist can use to his advantage, surely by all the rules of evidence he is free to do so. Certainly no reputable creationist will attempt to portray an evolutionist as supporting the case for creation. When proving a case, any piece of favorable evidence an attorney can pry out of a hostile witness is choice evidence indeed; the attorney would be remiss not to make the most of it. So with the creationist using statements of the evolutionist as evidence. Therefore, when a problem arises and is discussed in evolutionary writings, a creationist is justified in pointing out the problem as a weakness in the theory of evolution.

The quotations in this paper are from writings of those of the evolutionist persuasion unless the man's position is identified otherwise. In support of this point let us consider some words that William R. Thompson wrote in 1956:

> As we know, there is a great divergence of opinion among biologists, not only about the causes of evolution but even about the actual process. This divergence

exists because the evidence is unsatisfactory and does not permit any certain conclusion. It is therefore right and proper to draw the attention of the non-scientific public to the disagreements about evolution. But some recent remarks of evolutionists show that they think this unreasonable. This situation, where scientific men rally to the defense of a doctrine they are unable to define scientifically, much less demonstrate with scientific rigor, attempting to maintain its credit with the public by the suppression of criticism and the elimination of difficulties, is abnormal and undesirable in science.[6]

The statement that "everyone working in science accepts evolution as a fact" is often used as an argument for compelling acceptance of the evolutionary theory. This argument was again presented in an article by Ernst Mayr when he replied to Duane Gish's defense of creation as follows: "Frankly I do not know of a single well-informed person who questions the factuality of evolution." [7]

The following is a list of well-informed persons who have written from a creationist's point of view and whose writings show them to be reasonable and well-informed scholars: Thomas Barnes, director of the Schellinger Research Laboratory, also on the faculty of the University of Texas at El Paso; Duane Gish, biochemist at the Upjohn Laboratories, Kalamazoo, Mich.; George Howe, professor of biology, Westmont College, Calif.; Walter E. Lammerts, in the past on the faculty of the University of California and for many years research director of Germain's, in addition to being the leading rose authority on the West Coast; Frank L. Marsh, professor of biology at Andrews University; John Moore, professor of science education, Michigan State University; Henry Morris, formerly professor of hydraulic engineering and head of the civil engineering department, Virginia Polytechnic Institute; William R. Thompson, former director of the Commonwealth Institute of Biological Control, Ottawa, Canada; C. E. A. Turner, professor of chemistry, Surrey, England; and Louis Wolfanger, formerly professor of soil science, Michigan State University. Probably each of these individuals could in turn name an equally large and possibly more impressive circle of men with whom they are acquainted and who have serious questions about the actuality of evolution. On this list could also be placed the late Austin Clark of the U. S. National Museum; the late J. J. Duyvenne de Wit, formerly head of the zoology department, Orange Free State University; the late Paul Lemoine, curator of the Natural History Museum, Paris, France; and the late L. Merson-Davies, goldmedalist in geology, of England.

Finally, it should be noted that the Creation Research Society has more than 100 voting members who have earned Ph. D. degrees in science and accept creation. Certainly it would be presumptuous for anyone to arbitrarily judge all these men as uninformed and incompetent because they espouse creation. While it is true this number represents a minority opinion, this of itself does not make their creationist belief a false one.

Actually the only two possibilities regarding the origin of the living world are development by transformisms (evolution) or creation by God. Solly Zuckermann once wrote: "Either evolutionary change or miraculous divine intervention lies at the back of human intelligence. The second of these possibilities does not lend itself to scientific examination. It may be the correct explanation, but, from a scientific point of view, it cannot be legitimately resorted to in answer to the problem of man's dominantly successful behavior until all possibilities of more objective explanation through morphological, physiological and psychological observation and

41

experiment are exhausted.'' [8] Zuckermann thus delineates the reason why creation is unacceptable to many scientists.

The situation appears to be a little less biased in England since the *Journals of the Transactions of the Victoria Institute* were opened to discussion from both sides. Douglas Dewar's debates with J. B. S. Haldane and Shelton were published in England. Some recent publications from the continent, particularly in France and Germany, would seem to indicate that evolution-versus-creation can be more freely discussed. E. J. Corner wrote: ''Much evidence can be adduced in favor of the theory of evolution—from biology, biogeography and paleontology, but I still think that, to the unprejudiced, the fossil record of the plants is in favor of special creation.'' [9] Corner goes on to point out other deficiencies in the theory of evolution as applied to the plant world; nevertheless, even in the face of his earlier statement, he does not consider creation as a viable alternative but plaintively queries: ''And where else have we to worship?'' (Ibid.)

One could also raise the valid question as to whether books and articles favoring creation are scarce because the creationist view cannot get a fair hearing in our day. The position of science today is rather intolerant of dissenting views, as might be judged from the following examples.

Thompson mentioned in some correspondence that the chapter on evolution in his recently reissued work *Science and Common Sense* would have been much stronger against evolution were he to write it today. As he put it, at the time he wrote it the book had to be passed by a reader who had strong evolutionistic views. Therefore Thompson was forced to modify his own position to get the book published. In another recent letter he mentioned that Rev. H. St. Denis, dean of philosophy at the University of Ottawa, had five book reviews refused by the *University Review* on the grounds that they contained severe criticism of Teilhard de Chardin, the current idol of theistic evolutionists. Since then they have been published in the October 1965 issue of *Le Monde et la Vie.*

The case of Immanuel Velikovsky first came to my attention when I read the article by George Sokolsky, noted columnist, who wrote: "So it appears from what can be learned about it that certain scientists, including leading astronomers, threatened Macmillan with a boycott of their textbooks if they did not rid themselves of Professor Velikovsky's book. Of course, what the learned and liberal professors wanted really was a total suppression of a book which opposes their dogma." [10] Macmillan yielded to the threats, since they were an extensive publisher of textbooks, and transferred the publishing operations to Doubleday Doran Company, which does not publish science texts and therefore was immune to such a threat. Doubleday published all four of Velikovsky's books.

Reference can also be made to John Larrabee's article in the August 1963 issue of *Harper's* magazine, "Scientists in Collision: Was Velikovsky Right?" This should be required reading for all who maintain that scientists are completely objective and never biased. Larrabee points out that as early as 1950 Velikovsky predicted the high temperature of Venus, the radio emissions from Jupiter, as well as the phenomenon we know as the Van Allen radiation belts. For none of this has Velikovsky been given any credit on the basis of priority, nor have his predictions even been acknowledged in any of the descriptive writings on these matters. To avoid misunderstanding, I should mention that Velikovsky is not a creationist, although considered a scientific heretic of the first magnitude. Further, in this country almost all books dealing with creation that I know of have had to be published by religious book houses. Finally, the Library of Congress automatically classes any work with Creation in its title under the theological division.

The theory of evolution is based on a number of fundamental considerations. The first one to be briefly considered is classification, or taxonomy. This argument follows these lines: Since it is possible to classify organisms, it is held that all true classification should be genealogical. This basic assumption results in taxonomists repeatedly reshuffling classifications of plants and animals in an effort to find new natural systems of classification based on descent. Any current system of classification is therefore held to be natural and thus a proof of evolution. Frankly, that we can group living and fossil forms of life into some 30 animal phyla and some 25 plant divisions would be the last thing one should expect from an evolutionary development. A random evolutionary development should call for an enormous hodge-podge, rather than such a relatively small number of recognizable entities compared with the total species number. Although these major phyla and divisions are not as clear-cut as we might like them to be, yet they are stable and recognizable groups. Furthermore, that we can arrange animals and plants into groups on the basis of resemblances should be no more significant for developmental history than that we can arrange the elements into families. Have you ever heard a chemist propose that the halogen series evolved from fluorine to iodine because it is possible to arrange them in this series on the basis of similarities?

It is also pertinent to pose another question: Why should the type form insect or cephalopod continue to be inherited in the face of random variations, if transformism be true? Even in a lower hierarchical level, despite all repeated mutations, the majority of species and all genera are real entities. This was recognized by C. E. Davenport, who wrote: "When I study thrips and wish to secure a species described fifty or more years ago as living in a certain composite plant in eastern Russia, then if I go to the designated locality and look in the designated species of flower, I will find the species with all the characters described 50 or 100 thrip generations ago. How is such an experience to be harmonized with universal mutations?" [11] Davenport refers to this as the heart of the problem of evolution.

An evolutionist may say that when we find animals in nature grading in complexity of structure from a protozoan to a mammal, this proves that evolution from a one-cell to a multicellular form has taken place. The creationist says that a multiplicity of forms was part of the design of the Creator, with each occupying and filling an ecological niche. Both these statements are logical. Which is correct? Since this is subjective evidence (animals and plants don't carry classification labels), an argument could continue ad infinitum on this subject with no progress being made. The late Austin H. Clark, once curator of the U. S. National Museum, wrote: "It is almost invariably assumed that animals with bodies composed of a single cell represent the primitive animals from which all others are derived. They are commonly supposed to have preceded all other animal types in their appearance. There is not the slightest basis for this assumption beyond the circumstance that in arithmetic—which is not zoology—the number one precedes the other numbers." [12]

Second, comparative anatomy is considered an important part of the argument for evolution. A creationist and an evolutionist could stroll through a museum. One looks at the specimens displayed and holds that structural similarity in mammals, for example, suggests that all forms have evolved from a common ancestor. The other, seeing the same displays, believes that the structural similarities suggest a common general design to meet a common environment created by God. And again we reach an impasse. There is no empirically correct conclusion possible, since the evidence is subjective, depending on the belief of the individual using it.

However, a word of caution has to be injected here. To think of animals in terms of bones and dead bodies alone is not enough. Certainly, for example, the differences between cat and dog transcend the anatomical and physiological, since the temperaments of the two animals are different and represent an innate difference between these two animals. In making comparisons, particularly in discussing similarities, this aspect of dissimilarities is too often ignored. There is a procedural fallacy where, for example, one looks at an animal, names a certain bone, then looks at another animal and uses the same name for a corresponding part. By postulating the bone as being the same and therefore having phylogenetic significance, one now uses this as evidence. However, the similarity may be more in the nature of an interpretation, and hence a value judgment, rather than the empirical fact it is so often made out to be. The problem is further clouded by the presentation of simplified drawings with changed positions and scales, e. g., the aortic arches in vertebrates. Animal fossils are classified on the basis of skeletal parts solely, of necessity ignoring, since they are absent, such characteristics as warmbloodedness, the number of heart chambers, red blood cell structure, presence or absence of diaphragm, and the like.

A third proposed proof of evolution is that of vestigial organs. These are structures found in some animal or human organism that are considered to have no use in the present form, but they have had a use in previous forms and therefore represent a sort of memory of an evolutionary ancestor. Truly the fate of vestigial organs has been rather sad. There was once a long list of human organs that were considered as useless remnants of man's evolutionary past. Although this list once ran to about 180, today most of the list has gone the way of all flesh. In our day it seems odd to find that such structures as the tonsils, the parathyroids, the thymus, the pineal gland, the appendix, and the coccyx were all among those on the list considered to be vestigial. Certainly anyone who has suffered a broken coccyx is painfully aware of the fact that it serves as an anchorage for rectal muscles; obviously, if it is serving a useful function in the body, it cannot be a vestigial remnant. The appendix has now been admitted to play a part in the control of the intestinal flora, and again, since it has proved to have use, particularly in the light of recent observations made in connection with the growth of germ-free organisms, the appendix must be taken off the vestigial list. Tonsils and the various endocrine glands mentioned have long been classed as important and useful structures in the body of man. True, we can get along without our tonsils and we can get along without our appendix, but we can also get along without one arm and one leg, and certainly nobody in his right mind would for this reason class them as vestigial.

In the animal world the claws on either side of the vent in certain boas and pythons have often been pointed to as useless relics of the hind legs of snake ancestors. But Dewar refers to A. K. Martin, who wrote *The Ways of Man and Beast in India* and therein reports observing that these protuberances are of assistance in the movement of these snakes. Others have also referred to the fact that the spurs projecting from the python serve as a means of helping the animal anchor itself in movement through trees.

Two more examples should be mentioned: the semilunar fold in man and the transitory teeth of whales. The main function of the semilunar fold seems to be to collect foreign matter that gets into the eye and concentrate it into a sticky mass in the corner of the eye, where it can easily be removed. This has been reported by E. P. Stibbe.[13] With respect to the whales that have embryological teeth that never grow into teeth, Vialleton says: "Certain of these supposed vestigial organs deserve special examination, because they play a part that was unknown to Darwin. When he cited as truly vestigial organs the germs of teeth in the fetuses of whales devoid of teeth in the adult state, and those of the upper incisors in certain ruminants, the gums of which they never pierce, he forgot that these germs in mammals, where they are very large relative to the parts enclosing them, play a very important part in the formation of the bones of the jaws, to which they furnish a point on which these mold themselves. Thus these germs do have a function." [14] Furthermore, John Cameron reports that he studied a microcephalic idiot whose jaws receded because of poor tooth development. He says, "In many of these individuals the teeth never develop at all. The cause of poorly developed jaws are due to a deficiency or actual failure of development of the dental germs." [15]

In his *Transformist Illusion* Dewar insistently raises a rather pertinent question: Where are the nascent organs, those that are about to evolve into useful organs? I have not encountered anyone other than Darwin who has ever discussed or even mentioned this subject. Logically, if new organs are in the process of being developed, then in some animal form we should find some incompletely developed organs that are on the way to develop into fully useful structures later but at present have no function. Where is there any such evidence?

A fourth point is the evidence from embryology. Ernst Haeckel in 1866 enunciated the Law of Recapitulation, or Biogenetic Law, succinctly stated thus: "Ontogeny recapitulates phylogeny," or: The development of the individual repeats the development of his race. De Beer and Swinton refer to the Law of Recapitulation as "a theory that in spite of its exposure, its effects continue to linger in the nooks and crannies of zoology." [16] With respect to Sinnott and

Wilson's position that some leaves would seem to recapitulate an ancestral trait, De Beer and Swinton say that the Biogenetic Law cannot be applied here in view of the frequency with which young foliage leaves are found to be more specialized than those formed at later stages. The embryologist Huettner gave a fairly accurate picture of the light in which this has come to be viewed when he said: "As a law, this principle has been questioned, it has been subjected to careful scrutiny and has been found wanting. There are too many exceptions to it. However, there is no doubt that it contains some truth and that it is of value to the student of embryology." [17]

He proceeds further to point out some other difficulties. It had become necessary to divide the characteristics developed in an embryo into primitive (palingenetic) and specialized (coenogenetic) characteristics. Then it developed that there was a problem in differentiating between the two. Students of embryology complained that the palingenetic traits are obscured and sometimes eliminated at the expense of the coenogenetic. For example, there is never a true blastula or gastrula in the mammals. Furthermore, organs in many instances do not develop in the proper order. In the earliest fishes found, there are teeth but no tongues. But in the mammalian embryos, the tongue develops before the teeth. Huettner says there are numerous cases of this type of problem. It is known that environmental conditions will change the orderly sequence of differentiation in the embryo; this drives one to the conclusion that recapitulation must be subject to change. All this led Huettner to refuse to accept the recapitulation theory as a "law." It is also of interest to note that most crabs hatch out of a larval form known as zoeas, which differ greatly from the adult form. Yet other crabs hatch out as miniature crabs. Where is the operation of the Biogenetic Law in such instances? Abbreviated life cycles are known in many organisms, e. g., hydra versus many of the other coelenterates.

Again, embryologists who make phylogenies sometimes work at embarrassing cross purposes with paleontologists. In human development, it is noted, we find that most of the bones develop from embryonic cartilaginous foundations, for instance those that develop into the ethmoid, sphenoid, occipitals, as well as the vertebrae and the long bones of the forelimbs. As one grows older, more and more cartilage is replaced by bone. All this would seem to imply that cartilage is primitive and bone is more advanced. Applied to phylogenies, this would mean that sharks, as cartilaginous fish, would be the precursors of the bony fish. Unfortunately, if you take the paleontological record on its face value, we find, to our surprise, that the cartilaginous fish seem to have developed from the bony fish, since the latter occur earlier in the geological record.

In embryological development simpler parts must be formed before more complicated ones. In small embryos, shape will be determined by physical forces, which play less and less a part in determining shape as size increases. Many apparent recapitulations may only be expressions of the fact that all animals are built out of the same kind of materials such as carbohydrates, fats, proteins, etc. Often recapitulation is absurdly irrelevant. For instance, the respiratory surface develops late in an embryo, yet how could earlier forms have survived without it? The head size in the mammalian embryos is relatively enormous but very small in their ancestors.

Long ago, when I worked in embryology, it was pointed out that the embryo has two types of organs: (a) those that do not function until after the child is born, of which the lungs are a good example, and we therefore develop only one lung system; and (b) those that have a function during embryonic life as well as later, changing form, sometimes several times, to meet changing needs. I would consider the heart and the kidneys in this category. It might then be pointed out that successive kidneys, for example, rather than demonstrating recapitulation of ancestors, are meeting changing needs.

The question is often raised: What about the ability of scientists to create life? In these days we so often find a headline proclaiming "Scientists Create Life," only to discover that the progress toward this goal has been a crawl rather than the successful attainment of the goal.

A theory that purports to solve the riddle of the origin of life should start with the inorganic and wind up with at least a functioning cell. Intermediate steps would of necessity be the development of proteins and deoxyribonucleic acids (DNA), as well as the ribonucleic acids (RNA). These are all molecules of tremendous size but still organic molecules. They are not living, although they are associated with the growth and reproduction of living things.

Viruses essentially consist of a protein membrane or structure enclosing a core of nucleic acid. They multiply by invading the cells of an organism and using its cell constituents to produce additional viral units. One virus form invades bacteria and destroys them. These forms are known as the bacteriophages or simply phages. They have been the subject of much study, which forms the basis of much of our knowledge of viruses. In terms of origins, viruses are debatable organisms. Although there are those who hold that viruses are intermediate between the living and the nonliving, many agree with Frederick Bawden of England, noted virologist, who holds that they are degenerate forms of life.

Sol Spiegelman of the University of Illinois took a bacteriophage from Japan and isolated an RNA molecule from it. Then from another bacteriophage he also isolated a specific enzyme, replicase. When the two were placed in a nutrient material, other RNAs were produced. In this case the enzyme generated identical copies in the form of viral RNA. As in natural viruses, this new RNA can infect bacteria by serving as the template for additional viruses. Each enzyme recognizes the genome for its own RNA and requires it as template for synthesis. However, the presence of more than one nuclease will break down the whole procedure. So this process is simply duplicating some very complex viral chemistry. When Spiegelman was asked if he had created life in a test tube, he replied, "Only God can create life." [18] Another biochemist at the same time commented: "*If* we knew the chemical composition of each different molecule in the living cell and *if* we knew how they reacted, it would take us about 10 years to do what the living cell can do in 10 minutes." (Ibid.)

Stanley Miller first performed the experiment of passing an electric spark through a mixture of water, ammonia, and methane, producing a soup of simple amino acids. Later an electron beam was passed through such a mixture and produced the simple nitrogen base adenine. This base, classed as a purine, occurs in RNA along with another purine, guanine, as well as pyrimidines such as cytosine and uracil. Chemists then have also irradiated with ultraviolet light a mixture of water, ammonia, and methane to form formaldehyde, which was then polymerized by further radiation to form ribose and deoxyribose. These are the pentose sugars that occur in a typical nucleotide molecule.

An inorganic phosphate has been heated with a mixture of uracil and ribose to link these two compounds together to form diuridilic acid, which is a double-linked nucleotide molecule. All such experiments have been hailed as being the answer to how life originated. However, doing this sort of thing in the laboratory under carefully controlled conditions and having the same thing occur by chance in an open environment are two different things. Furthermore, these results are still a far cry from creating something living. These compounds are still only organic chemicals; complex, yes, and representing some beautiful syntheses, but such syntheses are not yet the creation of life.

But let's go back to the beginning of this discourse on the origin of life. Since the Urey-Miller experiment it is practically stated as fact that the earth had a beginning atmosphere of water, methane, and ammonia. This is an application of the "Law of Logical Necessity," which is of no value. An interesting article in *Science* [19] would seem to negate this theory concerning the primordial atmosphere. Three investigators, Martin Studier, Ryoichi Hayatsu, and Edward Anders, examined meteorites that showed hydrocarbon traces. These meteorites were assumed to have come from either comets or asteroids. The men examined the trapped gases within the bodies of these meteorites on the assumption that these trapped gases might indicate the gases present when the hydrocarbons were formed. The results were not at all comforting to devotees of the Urey-Miller conditions. Examination indicated that instead of the required ammonia, which was totally lacking, nitrogen was present. Another surprising discovery was the overwhelming preponderance of aromatic over aliphatic hydrocarbons. The carbohydrates and amino acids referred to before as being theoretical intermediates in the process of creating life are all basically aliphatic compounds or derived from them. None of these can be derived from aromatic compounds. Their presence would thus seem to mitigate against a Urey-Miller atmosphere. Also there was an absence of the heavier members of the methane series. To the authors this evidence seemed to exclude a process such as proposed by Urey and Miller for the origin of life by natural processes.

Another piece of evidence against the Urey-Miller scheme is the total absence of any evidence in the stratigraphic record of conditions other than those now pertaining. No matter how old the rocks are supposed to be, the Precambrian sedimentaries and metamorphics are composed of fragments of older rocks which seem to be the same as those now present.

William W. Rubey [20] in a discussion of Stanley Miller's paper on *Formation of Organic Compounds on Primitive Earth* was quoted as concluding that the ocean and the air were formed as products of degassing of the interior of the earth. Evidence for volcanic activity is found in the earliest rocks. Gases associated with present-day eruptions are water, carbon dioxide, nitrogen, carbon monoxide, hydrogen, and sulfur compounds. Condensation of such a mixture would lead to an atmosphere of carbon monoxide, nitrogen, hydrogen, and varying amounts of water and carbon dioxide. Where is Miller's ammonia, which is so vital to his scheme?

All this speculation then becomes good clean fun, and the chemistry furnishes examples of beautiful, clever syntheses of organic compounds — but with no life or near life yet having been created. Even if a system classifiable as living is ever synthesized, man will not have proved that this is the way the first synthesis was executed. He will only be mimicking the processes of nature; that is, he will be walking in the footsteps of the Creator.

The question in many minds at the moment is probably: What about geology and the fossil evidence? At the beginning of this phase of the presentation I would submit that the question of the age of the earth is independent of the question of creation versus evolution, and I will so treat them. A number of individuals will accept the geological calendar as commonly presented today, yet will not accept any part of the theory of evolution. One who fell in this category was Douglas Dewar, recognized as one of the most effective proponents of creation. This position is obvious in his *Transformist Illusion*, where he takes the geological calendar as read, but throughout the book he musters powerful arguments against evolution.

Although originally in his college years and for a while there-after Dewar was an evolutionist, as he became more knowl-edgeable in the morphology and physiology of birds he studied during his years in India, he more and more was con-vinced of the fallacy of the theory of evolution. His studies of birds were recognized to such a degree that several of his works are in the Graduate Library of the University of Michi-gan, for one. By the time he returned to England, he be-came one of the most effective voices of the protest against evolution.

Fossils are facts of life. The shells and bony structures that have been uncovered are real, as are such things as tracks, imprints, casts, and molds. So they must be dealt with as actualities and not as figments of the imagination. However, we will bear in mind that how they got to their resting place, under what circumstances they lived, as well as when they lived are all subject to interpretation and will result in dif-ferences of opinion. A beautiful and complete series of fossil shells may by some be considered to provide us with an excellent evolutionary series in which one form grades into another. However, such a change in shell structure may be simply an indication of a change in environment, for example, a more or less acid condition of the water. Cesare Emiliani has observed that temperature changes in the Gulf of Mexico seem to have affected the coiling of small protozoan shells from right to left. I was present when Professor Fagerstrom of the University of Nebraska reported that certain fora-miniferan forms altered their shells in response to pH changes in the water they were living in. So the very real question can be raised: Are these variations really evolutionary changes, or are they simply responses to environmental changes? What I wish to emphasize is that the evidence from paleontology is not absolutely conclusive and can never be so in itself, because it must always be incomplete. This is true not only because it may be geologically imperfect at any given time but because the picture it gives us of the organisms concerned is necessarily only a partial one.

Among the plants, the order of appearance of the fossils is anything but a progression from simplicity to complexity. In fact, in recent years, with the development of palynology (the study of microfossils in the form of spores in the rocks), the picture has become even more complex. According to the evolutionary theory we would expect to find liverworts and mosses following the algae as among the most primitive of plant forms since they are the simplest of all plants that are considered to be archegoniate. Unfortunately it has been observed that there is no geological evidence whatsoever that can make, for example, the delineation of the origin of bryophytes anything other than a hopeless one. A new field of study in paleontology is the application of palynology to the study of sedimentary deposits. This involves the study of fossil pollen grains or spores of plants. In many cases these are the only parts of the plant remaining as a fossil. Spores are sculptured uniquely, hence they can be compared and identified as to genus in many cases. Recent findings in this new field have thoroughly confused the evolutionary picture with respect to the plant world. Pollen grains have been found in Lower Devonian, Silurian, and Cambrian rocks; this would indicate the presence of vascular plants at the time of deposition of these rocks.

In addition to the presence of pollen grains, other difficulties have arisen. Mlle. S. Leclercq of the University of Liege, Belgium, reports: "A marked discrepancy observed between two floras so close in geological time as the Middle and Lower Devonian is difficult to reconcile. The absence in Lower Devonian of plant impressions positively related to any of the very differentiated plants of the Middle Devonian is astonishing." [21]

Daniel I. Axelrod also reports that the oldest land plants now known are from the early Cambrian of the Baltic region.[22] Pointing out that the bulk of the unmetamorphosed Paleozoic and Precambrian rocks are not continental but marine, Axelrod holds that few records of land plants would be expected in that period, at least so far as structures other than pollen grains would be concerned.

However, I would like to draw attention to the fact that the statements made by Axelrod relative to the distribution of the fossil plant forms and their environment apply with equal justice to the animal fauna. He points out the possibility that there were all sorts of land plants in existence that are not known as fossils because the sedimentary terrestrial deposits are not available. This, then, would imply that any missing terrestrial deposits, which might contain the structural fossils of plants, may also contain the fossils of land animals that once lived at the same time as such plant environments. Yet these animals, according to all current paleontological theories, would not have been evolved at that time. The only problem is that animals do not leave pollen grains, whereas plants do.[23]

It should be pointed out that nowhere do we find a complete record of deposition through all the geological ages. The complete geological record is made up by plugging in various segments of the record from various parts of the world so as to make up a whole geological column. But there is no locality anywhere on earth where you can dig down and uncover a complete geological column from end to beginning. Actually there is no locality where you can even uncover a complete series such as the horse, from *Equus* at the top to *Eohippus* or *Hyracotherium* at the bottom. Such a series must be made by drawing together fossils from different states, yes, even from other continents. A person committed to the theory of evolution might refuse to question a phylogenetic tree developed in this way. However, I submit that it is still open to debate. May not many of these forms have lived contemporaneously at different localities, or must the only acceptable explanation be that they succeeded one another? The answer is not carried on labels engraved on the fossils.

If you look at the complete picture of life in the rocks, you find some rather peculiar things. Probably one of the most important is the sharp break that occurs between the oldest rocks, known as the Precambrian, and the Cambrian rocks. Incidentally, all these fossils are aquatic. The first plants, on the basis of the remains, were algae. All the animals were invertebrates spread over all of the most important phyla, such as sponges, jellyfish, sea cucumbers, starfish, brachio- pods, mollusks, and crustaceans, as well as some worms. Thus, of the great divisions of the animal kingdom, we find that all have been formed by the Cambrian period except the verte- brates, and these appeared in the next, or Ordovician, period.

One very noticeable and important fact bearing on the theory of evolution: among these earliest fossils we find all the phyla appearing in the rocks fully formed, that is, possess- ing the complete bodily plan of construction typical of their phyla. For example, the earliest crustacea are undoubtedly crustacea, the earliest mollusks are undoubtedly mollusks, etc. As has been noted by any number of paleontologists, the phyla appeared separately, as it were, in most cases, giving among their fossils no indications of their origins from other phyla. If evolution were true, these phyla should have evolved one from the other in an increasing scheme of complexity and diversity. We should find them grading into one another. We should find fossils that connect the phyla unmistakably. But to date none have been found in the early rocks. Even when we deal with the vertebrates, a group that supposedly appeared last among the animals, we can find no true connecting link with previous invertebrate phyla.

The result is that there is no agreement regarding their origin. A search of the literature in the last 50 years will show that the vertebrates have been derived from nearly every one of the invertebrate groups, except possibly the protozoa. I think this sudden appearance of all the phyla without any transitional forms is a most powerful reason for negating a theory of evolution from amoeba, or unicellular form, to all the present various representative forms. Arnold Lunn once wrote: "Faith is the substance of fossils hoped for, the evidence of links unseen." [24]

Jepsen said: "These basic patterns obviously correspond to the complexes of morphological features characterizing the taxonomic categories from phyla down to genera (logically to species and even subspecies). The observed discontinuities between these patterns led many German morphologists in the 1930's to question the validity of the evolutionary theory, or to limit its operation to the confines of a given morphological type." [25] Since the geological record must always remain incomplete, such evidence can never prove the originality of the discontinuities. But this is certainly strongly suggested if we are limiting ourselves to facts and not to theory. Actually I would think that if the type of origin of new forms suggested by the known fossil record were to be named, it would of necessity be called origin by creation.

D. Dwight Davis in 1949 commented on the gaps in the geological record. He held that the sudden emergence of new types has given real trouble. He noted that many German morphologists question the validity of evolution, and both he and Simpson referred to such paleontologists as Schindewolf and Kuhn, who have felt this way. Davis also said: "The facts of paleontology conform equally well with other interpretations that have been discredited by neobiological work, for example, divine creation, innate developmental processes,

Lamarckism, etc., and paleontology by itself can neither prove nor refute such ideas" (Jepsen, pp. 64 ff.). I agree, but let it be noted that Davis still had faith in evolution.

Another difficulty of the fossil record is what might be termed "skipping." It was James D. Dana who mentioned land snails of the Carboniferous period. They disappeared from the record, not to reappear till the Cretaceous period, after which they persisted into present times. Dana also mentioned scorpions of the Upper Silurian, which then disappeared until the Carboniferous. At this time they return in the fossil record, along with spiders, which both disappear after the Cretaceous, not to reappear until the Tertiary period. In 1911 Smith mentioned the shrimp *Anaspida*, which has not been found as a fossil in any rocks since the Carboniferous but appeared in his day in mountain streams in remote Tasmania. Finally, you may recall the coelacanth, or lobe-finned fish, *Latimeria*, which belongs to a group that was thought to have become extinct in the Devonian period. From the Devonian to the present day not a single fossil of this form has been found in any rock. But by the end of 1958 nine had been caught in the ocean off the island of Madagascar. Incidentally, its present apparent deep-water habitat ought to cause some rethinking of the formation of rocks that contain lobe-finned fossils.

Of the early Paleozoic formations 90 percent of the rocks are depositions in shallow seas, with the remaining 5 percent those of coastal plains and deltas. We might well ask: Where is the record of the land? What plants and what animals lived on the land at that time? In view of the findings of palynology regarding spores of vascular plants in the Cambrian, these become even more legitimate questions. However, all the paleontological reconstructions seem to be confined to marine environments. Through the late Paleozoic the percentage distribution isn't much different.

In the Mesozoic we find plenty of reptiles, since we have in these rocks a greater percentage of terrestrial deposits, which represents their environment. But does this necessarily mean that there were no reptile forms living through much of the Paleozoic on the same land that was supporting the growth of the plants that produced the spores? I am fully aware that what I have just said is paleontological heresy.

I am bothered by the insistence on the principle that "the present is the key to the past" and the principle of either uniformity or uniformitarianism. When I look at deposits such as the bone beds at Agate Springs in western Nebraska, which consist of a remarkable number of various mammals whose bones have become completely disjointed and are one big jumbled-up mess that reaches a layer 5 to 6 feet thick, I ask myself: How could this have come about? Note also the islands consisting of almost sheer bones that are described as existing in the sea north of Siberia. Include also the quick and sudden burial of lions and mammoths in Alaska, now being uncovered by gold mining operations. I am bothered by densely packed layers of shells alternating with almost completely fossil-free layers found in the Greenhorn limestone in Kansas and Nebraska. Above all I am disturbed by the cyclothem explanations in all the geology books to explain the coal beds, and then I find innumerable cases of tree trunks fossilized or coalified, which pierce through successive layers in lengths of tens of feet. And I could give many more instances. Even though catastrophism is a dirty word for all geologists, I am afraid that for me these instances and others that I could add spell catastrophe rather than slow, even deposition.

I am bothered when I read glib descriptions of equable paleoclimates over the whole world in terms of our present-day solar relationships. I know that when you have a spherical body interposed in the path of parallel energy rays, you can't escape a climatic zonation because of the sphericity. There is some factor here that is not taken into account.

I am disturbed when paleomagnetism is airily referred to and complete reversals of the earth's magnetic field are postulated, which seem to be supported by sound evidence. But I ask myself: What kind of circumstances brought this about? Above all, what kind of associated phenomena have been completely left out of consideration? What conceivable force could have reversed the whole magnetic field of the earth? We know that the radiation belts are involved in such a field, but what kind of storms would have accompanied such a reversal? What would have been the effect on living organisms at that point in reversal where the earth's magnetic field was at zero strength?

It is questions such as these and the failure to find reasonable answers that drive me to suspend judgment on the picture painted in texts dealing with past conditions. I have no quarrel with the various rock layers as diagramed in texts. If there has been drilling of wells along a line drawn across several states, the cores would present factual evidence as to how this part of the earth's upper crust is composed. But I may be pardoned if I express considerable skepticism when a set of quite unnoticed activities is postulated as the means whereby these various layers were formed and laid down.

A final question that is probably in the minds of many: What about human evolution? From the evolutionist's point of view, man has evolved from an ape form known as *Ramapithecus*. This form has been found in India in the Siwalik Hills. Current opinion would seem to hold that this form is dated as Miocene. The only material currently available seems to be jaw and tooth fragments. From this point on to the rock level known as the Late Pliocene-Pleistocene, there is very little to go on so far as fossil evidence is concerned. In explanation it is held that the habits of anthropoids do not favor fossilization. In this connection Ernst Mayr has some interesting things to say. "Logically it is possible to conceive of a situation in which we would be certain that man has evolved [from the primates] but [we] would know nothing about the actual history of this evolution." From a standpoint of faith in evolution, Mayr says: "Our not very remote ancestors were animals, not men." On the other hand, speaking from the scientific standpoint, Mayr also says: "Man's recent history is shot through with uncertainties." And on the same page he adds: "There is not merely one missing link" but a "whole series of grades of missing links in hominid history." [26]

There has been a profound change in outlook on the subject of sequence of human fossils. All human fossils today are put into one genus: *Homo*. This is correcting a rather unfortunate habit in the past that resulted in far more generic names than were justified. Dobzhansky says on this matter: "A minor but rather annoying difficulty for a biologist, is the habit human paleontologists have of flattering their egos by naming each find a new species, if not a new genus. This causes not only a needless cluttering of the nomenclature but it is seriously misleading because treating as a species what is not a species beclouds some important issues." [27] The result of the compression is that a common current classification groups all hominid fossils into the following three categories. The first is *Homo transvaalensis*. This group is more commonly referred to as the two *Australopithecus* species, either *africanus* or *robustus*. The second form is known as *Homo erectus*. This form has two varieties: *erectus* (Java man) and *pekinensis* (Pekin man). The final form is *Homo sapiens*. This form also has two varieties: *neanderthalensis* and *sapiens*.

The second and third forms have all been placed in the same genus, *Homo,* and referred to as hominids because they all show upright carriage, bipedal locomotion, and essentially human tooth and jaw structure. This question of what is a human being, particularly when you are dealing with just the skeletal parts, is somewhat of a problem. It should never be forgotten that you are dealing mostly with incomplete remains. It is generally assumed arbitrarily that if there is evidence of controlled use of fire and the use of tools accompanying the remains, then such remains ought to be classed as human. There is always the interesting question: Were these tools and fire used by the fossil forms present, or were these used by another form that coexisted with the fossil form, but of whom no fossils have as yet been found?

Behavior cannot be discerned in man's ancestry, for behavior leaves no bones. I think anthropologists are wary today of equating size of brain and quality. The brain size varies among all mammals. It certainly varies in human beings. The average capacity of the modern American man is held to be about 1,400 cubic centimeters. Yet Anatole France had a brain capacity of 1,000 to 1,200 cubic centimeters. Jonathan Swift had a brain capacity twice as great. Manifestly we would not be justified in concluding that Swift was twice as intelligent, since what we know of the two men does not justify this statement. It is generally agreed today that the brain capacity of *Homo sapiens* will usually range from somewhere close to 1,200 to about 1,500 cc., whereas Neanderthal man ran as an average in excess of this, generally having a larger brain than modern man. His range, however, was from 1,300 to 1,425 cc. *Homo erectus pekinensis* specimens range in brain capacity from 900 to 1,200 cc., and *Homo erectus* runs from 770 to 1,000 cc.

In the *Australopithecus africanus* forms the brow ridges are heavy but no more so than in some fossil and even a few modern skulls. The mastoid process is present, and it is conical as in man. This is considered to be of assistance in anchoring the muscles that hold the skull erect, and therefore it is assumed that the Australopithecines had a human rather than an apelike neck. However, the brain size seems to have run about 450 to a speculative 600 cc. If you take the 550 maximum, which is the average estimate of most anthropologists, then you have what Henri Vallois, the noted French anthropologist, calls a Rubicon, and this 200-cc. gap (from 550 to 770) has not been crossed by any fossils to date.

Not too long ago it was rather firmly held that there was a direct line of human evolution running from some unknown anthropoid precursor to the Australopithecines to Java and Peking man to Neanderthal to Cro-Magnon to modern man. This beautiful phylogenetic line has fallen by the wayside. Several factors have contributed to its demise. It has recently been admitted by Robinson, Leakey, and others that the Australopithecines can no longer be viewed as the oldest known relatives of *Homo sapiens,* because more human (less brutalized) forms have been discovered who lived simultaneously with them. It was in 1963 that Leakey reported the find of a human pre-Zinjanthropus form which he named *Homo habilis.* At that time he suggested that all works on anthropology would have to be rewritten, including his own, since *Homo habilis* for practical purposes was very similar to modern man. Furthermore, Brown and Robinson in 1949 discovered some human remains in Swartkrans. These consisted of two mandibles (lower jawbones). J. T. Robinson of the Transvaal Museum at Pretoria, South Africa, has written an opinion of this discovery, which he named *Telanthropus.* He claims they were a superior race, definitely human. After invading the sites where the more inferior South African Australopithecines lived, this race brought about their extinction by the more intelligent manufacture and use of weapons. R. J. Mason,[28] a research officer of the Archaeological Survey of the Republic of South Africa, is of a similar opinion. Carleton Coon also refers to *Telanthropus* as human. Certainly if these human forms were contemporary with *Australopithecus,* it is unlikely the latter could be the ancestor.

One of the most fascinating developments also has been the finds of Neanderthals in the caves of Skhul and Tabun at Mount Carmel. In Skhul you find more modern forms apparently predating the classical Neanderthal type. While the Tabun population was being specialized in a Neanderthal direction, the Skhul population was remaining less specialized. The literature today has frequent reference to Neanderthaloids, who were the ancestors of the classic Neanderthal men and also more modern in feature. Hence, far from his being man's ancestor, most anthropologists today consider Neanderthal a variety of *Homo sapiens* that became a dead end. Nevertheless, there is also increasing evidence supporting the degree of "civilization" of Neanderthal, e. g., the finding of whole Neanderthal villages in the south of Russia.[29] This has led the French paleontologist Jean Piveteau to state: "Being torn from the same layer as *Homo sapiens,* he [Neanderthal man] suffered, in his body, *a veritable regression;* but one recovers in the psyche of this physically degraded man the mark of his human origin" (italics mine).[30] In this same work Piveteau makes a statement on page 50 that is being held by a number of other individuals and has previously been referred to: that the dimensions of the brain cannot furnish any indication whatsoever as to its functioning. It should also be mentioned that the possibility exists that deleterious gene mutations and recombinations could bring about a decrease in brain size, even tending towards microcephaly. These changes would also bring about facial feature changes. Certainly these possibilities ought to be considered.

What are we then to do with this material on human evolution, of which I have given just the bare sketch? To deny the existence of the fossils is wrong. They do exist.

However, we can look at these now, in the light of the evidence from the Neanderthal situation, at Skhul and Tabun, and ask ourselves: Are these animals on the way to being men? Or are these men who have been excessively brutalized and degenerated, actually a sort of devolution, that resulted finally in extinction? This latter view is the considered opinion of Dr. de Wit, who was head of the department of zoology at the University of the Orange Free State, Republic of South Africa. It is true that this overall application of the Neanderthal proposition is not subscribed to by the vast majority of paleontologists. However, it might be pointed out that prior to the discoveries of Skhul and Tabun any supposition that Neanderthal was a degenerate form of more modern human types would have been laughed out of existence. So we are faced again with the situation: Here is the evidence. Which way shall it be interpreted?

The Word of God Today

Paul A. Zimmerman, B. D., Ph. D.

Introduction: Challenges to the Inspiration of the Bible

The Lutheran Position on Scripture

The purpose of this essay is to review current attacks on the inspiration and veracity of the Bible and to strengthen faith in the conviction that the Bible is indeed God's Word and God's truth. Special attention is to be given to the opening chapters of Genesis. It may seem strange to some that it is necessary to do this. After all, the constitution of The Lutheran Church—Missouri Synod indicates under Article II that: "Synod, and every member of Synod, accepts without reservation: 1. The Scriptures of the Old and the New Testament as the written Word of God and the only rule and norm of faith and of practice; 2. All the Symbolic Books of the Evangelical Lutheran Church as a true and unadulterated statement and exposition of the Word of God." [1] Moreover, the Formula of Concord (Solid Declaration, Rule and Norm) states: "We pledge ourselves to the prophetic and apostolic writings of the Old and New Testaments as the pure and clear fountain of Israel, which is the only true norm according to which all

teachers and teachings are to be judged and evaluated."
And: ". . . the Word of God is and should remain the sole
rule and norm of all doctrine, and that no human being's
writings dare be put on a par with it, but that everything must
be subjected to it." [2]

The Presbyterians: New Confession for an Old One

Nonetheless we face differences of opinion about the
Bible and Biblical interpretation today. Within the Christian
church there are very few who in so many words deny that
the Holy Scriptures are authoritative in doctrine and in direc-
ting our lives. The questions rather are usually put this way:
In what respect are the Scriptures the Word of God? How do
we interpret the Scriptures and understand them properly?
These questions, in themselves valid, have called forth some
very interesting and frequently invalid answers.

For example, the General Assembly of the United
Presbyterian Church has produced a new confession. In the
introduction to its statement on Holy Scriptures we read:

> "This section is an intended revision of the West-
> minister doctrine, which rested primarily on a view of
> inspiration and equated the Biblical canon directly
> with the Word of God. By contrast, the pre-eminent
> and primary meaning of the word of God in the Con-
> fession of 1967 is the Word of God incarnate. The
> function of the Bible is to be the instrument of the
> revelation of the Word in the living church. It is not a
> witness among others but the witness without parallel,
> the norm of all other witness. At the same time ques-
> tions of antiquated cosmology, diverse cultural in-
> fluences, and the like, may be dealt with by careful
> scholarship uninhibited by the doctrine of inerrancy
> which placed the older Reformed theology at odds
> with advances in historical and scientific studies." [3]

This issue has caused a great stir among conservative laymen and theologians in the Presbyterian Church. It is typical of the modern approach to the Holy Scriptures, in which the Bible is often said to contain the Word of God or in which it is said that one meets the Word of God. We note specifically the refusal to equate the Holy Scriptures with the Word of God.

The Issue Stated

Perhaps another example will help make the problem clearer. The issue frequently becomes more lucid when it comes to focus on the creation stories of Genesis. The magazine *Resource* (March 1963, p. 11) contains an article entitled, "What Shall We Do With the Creation Stories?" The opening words read: "Is the Bible literally God's Word, given to us through men who automatically transcribed everything God said to them? Or does the Word of God come to us through the words of men? Are there portions of the Bible which are uninspired? Are there portions of the Bible which bring us God's truth in parable form, portions in which the essential message is true even though the outward facts can be questioned?" We note here the challenging of the inspiration of the entire Bible. We notice also the assumption that some of the facts recorded in the Bible may be in error. Again, this is symptomatic of a modern approach to the Bible which is very common.

Missouri's Preliminary Response

Many of the questions concerning revelation, inspiration, and the inerrancy of the Bible have also been of concern to those who teach, preach, and worship in The Lutheran Church—Missouri Synod. It is no secret that there have been some individuals who have strongly dissented with the established position of The Lutheran Church—Missouri Synod on verbal inspiration and related matters. Because of this, at the

Cleveland convention in 1962 the Missouri Synod established a Commission on Theology and Church Relations. Many of the questions we shall talk about have been referred to the commission. The commission produced a "Study Document on Revelation, Inspiration, and Inerrancy" which was presented to the church for study and reaction. After receiving the reactions, the committee declared at the Detroit convention in 1965: "That document has now served its purpose and is no longer before the church for action." The commission then presented to the convention a partial revision which it indicated was "not attempting to write a dogmatic treatise but rather to indicate the *limits* within which and the *lines* along which our *common* study of these issues should move and so give *stimulus* and *direction* to a concerted investigation of the problems on the part of all members of our Synod." [4] The Synod encouraged the synodical constituency to study and evaluate this statement and to present any reactions to the Commission on Theology and Church Relations. The Synod further resolved that the commission be directed to "complete its study of revelation, inspiration, and inerrancy in connection with its comprehensive study on hermeneutics [Scriptural interpretation] for submission to a later convention of the Synod." [5]

The "Revision of the Study Document on Revelation, Inspiration, and Inerrancy" is found on pages 292 – 95 of the *Proceedings* of the Detroit convention. It is a rather brief and admittedly incomplete document. It calls attention to the creative power of the Holy Spirit, who "lived and worked in prophets and apostles." It also states that we "recognize that the Spirit of power is at work in and through these words now when they are read, spoken, preached, or sung. We know that the inspired word is a divinely created Word, not a word produced by men but a word given by God." The authenticity of the message is attested by the statement: "Because the

Spirit speaks in the apostles, their witness to Jesus Christ is not a mere report about Him; rather, their witness confronts the world with Christ and through Him convicts the world of sin and righteousness and judgment." The statement reaffirms verbal inspiration and indicates that the church does not teach mechanical inspiration. It says: "We see also that the divine control of the apostle or prophet is not limited to the moment of the inspired writing but involves also God's governance of the man's whole previous history. The Spirit working in and through prophet and apostle takes the whole man, with all that his history has given him and made of him, into His service and moves him to speak 'from God' (2 Peter 1:21)." There is also a brief section on the inerrancy of the Scriptures, where it says: "The Lutheran Symbols [confessions] confess the inerrancy of the Scriptures with simple and forceful words: 'They will not lie to you' (Large Catechism, V. 76, in *The Book of Concord,* ed. Tappert, p. 455 . . .). The witness of Scripture in all its parts in their intended sense is true and wholly reliable. These words of the Scriptures are inerrant because they are inspired by God—words taught by the Holy Spirit, written by men moved by the Holy Spirit. These inspired words in all their various forms are the word of God. They are true and will not lead astray, but will accomplish the purpose for which God gave them."

The Current Scene in Theology

Before we can profitably estimate some of these issues which disturb our church in connection with the inspiration of the Bible, we need to look at the theological scene, particularly in Europe and in our own country. For what happens in Protestantism and Christianity both abroad and in this country influences our thinking in The Lutheran Church—Missouri Synod. Moreover, the observation of the results which different approaches to Scripture have produced can serve a most useful historical lesson. For we are sometimes invited to adopt one or another of these approaches and to depart from the position we presently hold.

Such an overview as we propose is indeed difficult to present. Even among various exponents of a certain theological position there is always a great deal of variety. Moreover, theologians are constantly changing their position. Then there is the danger of oversimplification. Many of the terms that must be used are technical. Nonetheless, we shall do our best under the Lord's guidance.

The Twentieth Century:
Liberalism, Neoorthodoxy, Biblical Theology,
Post-Barthian Liberalism

The June and September 1964 (Vol. XXXV) issues of the *Concordia Theological Monthly* carry an article by Dr. K. Runia, a Reformed professor of systematic theology in Australia. This excellent article is entitled "Dangerous Trends in Modern Theological Thought." It is useful reading for anyone who wants a summary of theological developments during the first 6 decades of this century. Runia indicates that it is common to divide the last 60 years into four phases. The first phase is that of liberalism and modernism. This was the time of a very optimistic view of man, a view which did not accept the Biblical doctrine of original sin. It was a time of emphasis on religious experience and the social gospel. It is commonly conceded that liberalism and modernism went into decline largely as a result of World War I, which did much to dispel the evolutionistic optimism about man and his perfectibility that was characteristic of so much of that theology.

But a new movement known as neoorthodoxy came into being under the leadership of Karl Barth, the famous Swiss theologian. It was called "orthodoxy" because it took more seriously the depravity of man, the importance of the

73

Biblical message, and various other aspects of orthodox Christianity. It was called "neo," or new, because it was not really a return to orthodox Christianity. Runia points out that it was a combination of diverging theologies and included some theologians who were somewhat on the right wing, such as Barth and Brunner, some who were far to the left (e. g., Tillich and Bultmann), and others who occupied an intermediate position (e. g., the Niebuhr brothers).

Another new development is called Biblical theology. This movement emphasizes a more serious view of Scripture and a rediscovery of the Biblical message, the "kerygma" or "herald's message" of God's redeeming grace in Christ. Runia points out that Biblical theology, however, does not abandon the concern for historical criticism of the Bible. But he indicates that it does give more attention to the unified presentation of the Bible's religious message (June 1964, pp. 331 — 32). However, talking about these somewhat more conservative scholars, John Warwick Montgomery makes the observation that "even the most orthodox of these theologians balk at an unqualified, objective identification of the historical Scripture with God's Word." [6]

Runia indicates that today we have entered a new phase, which is sometimes called post-Barthian liberalism. This is distinguished by two particular features. First, it accords to human reason a function in the reception of revelation; the interpreter of Scripture actually brings something to Scripture as well as takes something away from it. Second, its prime aim is to relate the Christian message to secular truth and to formulate this secular truth in terms relevant to the existing situation. (June 1964, p. 332)

Existentialism — Philosophical Roots of the New Theology

It may be helpful to look at the most recent developments in the approach to Scripture from the viewpoint of their philosophical undergirding. It is generally conceded that a great deal of the philosophical background can be traced to what is known as existentialism, sometimes called encounter philosophy. Sören Kierkegaard, in the last century, reacted against the sterile rationalism of the theology based on the philosophy of Hegel. Kierkegaard also opposed the general hypocrisy and dead intellectual Christianity of his day. He cried out for what has been called "a passionate individual decision" (in itself a good and necessary part of Christianity). However, he went on to hold that true religion really does not consist in understanding anything but is a matter of feeling. He stated: "If one asks objectively about the truth, one is reflecting subjectively about the relation of the individual; if only the How of this relation is in truth, then the individual is in truth, even though he is thus related to untruth." [7] That is, content of faith is secondary to sincerity of faith.

Another forerunner of existentialism was the German philosopher Nietzsche, who was the first to popularize the expression "God is dead." It is also the basic stance of the German philosopher Heidegger, who influenced Rudolf Bultmann, of whom we shall speak in a few moments. Existentialism has been labeled an anti-intellectual movement. It places little emphasis or importance on content, but centers on "encounter." When translated into theology, this means that the important thing is that you have an experience and encounter with God in reading the Word or studying it. It also means that the content of Scripture in terms of any propositional truth it may contain is either of no consequence or possibly in error. This has led in some cases to denial of belief in a soul, a future life, a resurrection, an absolute morality, etc. It is necessary to remember that many, many modern theologians are very strongly influenced by this philosophy.

Runia, in the September 1964 *Concordia Theological*

Monthly, points out that "Barthian theology never satis-
factorily solved the problem of the *authority of God's Word,*"
despite the fact that the Bible "had the central place in
Barth's and Brunner's theology." For them "the Bible *is* not
the Word of God in the sense of a direct identification, but
it has again and again to *become* the Word of God" (p. 479).
This is essentially an existential approach, although Barth
had some grave criticisms of existential philosophy. The idea
is that in encountering the Word it becomes the Word of God
for you. This implies that the Bible itself is not to be identified
with the Word on an equal basis and that it contains human
errors.

The "New Hermeneutic"

The topic that holds the stage today is the question of
the so-called "new hermeneutic," a new approach to Scriptural interpretation. One cannot consider the new hermeneutic
without mentioning Rudolf Bultmann. He is by no means the
only player on the stage. However, it is difficult to under-
estimate the influence he has had on modern theology, both
directly and through his students. Rudolf Bultmann is also
one of the fathers of the school of Gospel research known
as Form Criticism *(Formgeschichte).* Form Criticism is a study
of the assumed component units of the tradition which
allegedly underlies the synoptic gospels. In 1931 Bultmann
published *The History of the Synoptic Tradition.* Another work
from that time is titled *The Study of the Synoptic Gospels.*
This essay is significant because it reveals Bultmann's basic
presuppositions. He believes that the gospels are the product
of the Christian community. Although they may reflect
Christ's teaching, "one may admit the fact that for no single
word of Jesus is it possible to produce evidence of its authenticity." [8] Bultmann goes on to say that we can be certain that
there are some words in the gospels which Christ probably
said, but that one cannot be sure. He claims the gospels are

filled with legends and other additions put in by the early church. It is obvious that Bultmann offers an approach to the gospels which completely denies any possibility of divine inspiration by the Holy Spirit in the sense in which we understand it in classical Christianity.

Another characteristic of Bultmann's approach to Scripture is that he has a closed world view which he takes from modern science and which he places as a stricture on anything in Scripture. He believes that the Bible contains a mythical picture of the world as a three-storied structure, that it reflects the erroneous world views of the early Christians. He would also include in this the whole concept of miracles. Bultmann considers also the resurrection of Christ to be a myth. He considers these myths to be an attempt to say something religious, but he believes that they do not actually point to anything that took place. It is said that this development came into prominence about 1941 when he delivered a lecture on "The New Testament and Mythology." [9]

Present-day proponents of the new hermeneutic are heavily dependent on Rudolf Bultmann. When we talk about Scriptural interpretation or hermeneutics, we talk about exegesis. This term means the exposition of the Bible. In his essay "Is Exegesis Without Presuppositions Possible?" [10] Bultmann indicates that although exegesis must not decide what its results are going to be ahead of time, it must lean heavily on the method of historical critical research, including a view of the universe that rules out miracles and sees the "whole historical process as a closed unity." Montgomery indicates that Bultmann also speaks of "an existential 'life relation' between Scriptural text and the interpreter himself; thus all Biblical interpretation involves a necessary circularity" (p. 80). This is called the " 'hermeneutical circle' embracing text and exegete." In this sense, no exegesis or Scriptural interpretation can really be regarded as objective.

Montgomery points out that the post-Bultmannians, the exponents of the new hermeneutic, have changed some of Bultmann's conclusions as well as his approach, but that, nonetheless: "Though they have departed from their master in many respects, they all maintain the centrality of Bultmann's 'hermeneutical circle' and his conviction that an objective identification of the Biblical text with God's Word is a manifestation of unfaith" (p. 82). What this means is that the interpreter brings something to Scripture and that this influences what he gets out of it. It also means that he does not hope to find in Scripture any religious information in the sense of statements of positive truth. Rather it is an existential encounter and, as such, highly subjective.

The approach of the new hermeneutic makes very clear that it is a radical departure from the hermeneutics or method of interpreting Scripture used in the past. The historical development of the new hermeneutic has been reviewed by James Robinson.[11] He says: "When one opens Ernst Fuchs's *Hermeneutik* [1954, a systematic statement of the new hermeneutic], aware that it is the first New Testament hermeneutic since Torm's *Hermeneutik des Neuen Testaments* a quarter of a century before, the contrast between the two works is so overpowering that one is inclined to conclude that they belong to completely different fields and only by mistake came to share the name *Hermeneutik*." Robinson states that hermeneutics traditionally is the theory of exegesis or of Scriptural interpretation, but that the new hermeneutic is much more than this. It is basically a different approach to Scripture. It amounts to an "understanding." It involves basic presuppositions about Scripture itself and also what is known as *Sachkritik*. This is a German term which means a criticism of the content of Scripture. Perhaps no other expression more clearly points out that the text of God's Word is regarded as something which the interpreter may judge, rather than as something which judges him. The concept of the hermeneutical circle means that the interpreter must bring his presuppositions to the text before it can speak to him. Thus objective exegesis is impossible. Bultmann is said to have replaced *Heilsgeschichte* with *Heilsgeschehen*. *Heilsgeschichte* means a history of salvation; *Heilsgeschehen* means the saving event. In other words, once again, there is no historical account in Scripture in the sense that we think of history as a reliable account of actual events. Rather, interpreting it is itself an event which takes place now in a sense independently of what went on before. Among the most prominent of Bultmann's followers are the Germans Gerhard Ebeling and Ernst Fuchs. Fuchs is said to have gone beyond Bultmann by speaking in terms of a language event or *Sprachereignis*. Ebeling speaks in terms of a word event rather than a language event, or a *Wortereignis*.

It is extremely significant that the philosophical foundations of the new hermeneutic founded by the German philosophers Dilthey and Heidegger have, in the opinion of many, been effectively challenged by a philosopher at the University of Heidelberg, Hans Georg Gadamer. Gadamer appears to be reacting against existentialism and the emphasis on psychologism. He indicates that it is important to return to language and its subject matter. This seems to be a revolt against the claim of the new hermeneutic that propositional revelation is not important. Gadamer holds that the historic relation must ultimately be understood as a relationship of meaning that basically transcends the experiential horizon of the individual. He objects to the judging of history by the interpreter which is characteristic of the new hermeneutic. He says: "In reality history does not belong to us but we to it." (Robinson and Cobb, p. 70). Robinson characterizes this further by saying: "It is this dialectic between language and its subject matter *(Sprache* and *Sache)* rather than that between mythological language and the existential self-understanding it objectifies, which designates the point at which the hermeneutical discussion in Germany now stands'' (p. 77). Certainly this would seem to be a step in the direction of a saner view of the interpretative task.

A Response to the Challenge

The question being raised in our church today is: "How much of this new theology shall we buy?" What reliance shall we place on historical criticism, some of which is so radical as to destroy the concept of the inspiration of the Old and New Testament? Shall we say that the Bible may contain God's Word but also contains human words and human errors?

What then should we respond? Certainly we must abide by the Christian and Lutheran principle that the Scriptures are God's Word and the only source and norm of our doctrine. Certainly we must repudiate the theology of those who are led to deny inspiration and to deny that we may know anything in fact about what Jesus really said and did. Certainly we will not hesitate to classify as unchristian and heretical those who deny miracles, the authority of Christ, the divinity of Christ, and His resurrection. Certainly we will be aware of the great peril attached to any method or approach to Scripture that leads to the repudiation of everything Christianity stands for. Certainly we will not fall into the trap of believing that science has made it impossible for us to believe in the supernatural. For, by definition, science deals only with the natural. As such it is neither in a position to affirm or to deny the supernatural or the acts of a transcendent God who acts in history, speaks to prophets, and performs miracles through His Son and those to whom the power is given.

The Positive Results of Biblical Scholarship

Nonetheless, as we consider modern developments in theology, there is a haunting fear that perhaps the Bible is not the reliable, inspired rule of faith and life that we have thought it to be. Fundamentally the authority of God's Word and its defense is carried by the power of the Holy Spirit speaking in the Word itself. Of this we shall very soon reassure ourselves by looking at some of the many passages which reaffirm this and speak with authority. However, it may be instructive at this time to point to some of the positive results of modern scholarship which serve to illustrate the faithfulness of the Bible in those areas where it is tangent with history.

First of all, may we point to an article by Donald T. Rowlingson. He deals with the question of the so-called "search for the historical Jesus"; that is, Is it possible to know anything authentic about what Jesus really said and did? He concludes concerning the authenticity of the "remembrances" of the words and acts of Jesus in the Gospels that despite *Formgeschichte* and *Redaktionsgeschichte* "the Gospel portraits bear the authentic mark of a valid memory. . . . The person who is portrayed coheres, in forms of thought and speech and in every other way, to the first-century Palestinian milieu." [12] In plain language, the Gospels give every evidence of being reliable in their witness of Christ.

Rowlingson continues by criticizing the existentialism of Bultmann, Fuchs, and Ebeling. He says: "This trend of thought tends to operate in a cultural vacuum and on the basis of a questionable dualism which distinguishes too rigidly between *Historie* and *Geschichte* [that is, actual history and a vague type of religious account], with more attention to the subjective mechanics of interpretation than to the content and substance of faith" (p. 333). In plain language, he faults them for overemphasis on the interpreter's ideas and for neglect of the content of the Gospels. Here, then, is one theologian who cuts through the jungle of speculation and indicates that, after all, the Gospels still do stand as authentic witnesses to the words and acts of Christ.

In another article Robert Boling of McCormick Theological Seminary reviewed a translation and commentary on Genesis by a Jewish scholar, E. A. Speiser. This is the Anchor Bible translation. Boling points out that Speiser has indicated that there is a surprising amount of correlation between Genesis and what we have learned from archaeology. Boling says: ''We are provided with authentic reflections of periods, places, and institutions which cannot be squared with the assumption that the patriarchal narratives represent later Israel's projection of the world she knew back into the period of the fathers. The patriarchs are shown again and again to have done what in fact people did in the age of the finds of Mari, Nuzi, and elsewhere. Speiser argues with convincing examples that Israel's oral tradition preserved strikingly faithful memories of institutions and customs long after some of them no longer were understood in terms of their original setting. The section-by-section commentary adds up to a comprehensive corrective to the low view of patriarchal tradition that lingers still as a carry-over from nineteenth-century scholarship.'' [13] Again, the historical accuracy of the Old Testament is attested!

In an unpublished conference paper the Presbyterian Hebrew scholar Edward Young points out that the finds of archaeology have strongly substantiated the historical statements of the cultural background of the Pentateuch. He calls attention, for example, to the Horites, mentioned in Genesis 14. Once they were claimed to be nonhistoric; now they have been shown to be the Hurrians, a people who really existed. He also points out that the way Abraham took Hagar as a wife in order to raise up a child, since Sarah was childless, followed the Hurrians' practice. This did not make it moral, but it was the standard practice of the people who lived about Abraham.

The essentially historic framework of the Gospels has also been substantiated. For example, some have claimed the Gospel of St. John to be symbolic and of little historical value. Thus, in connection with the healing of the cripple by the pool of Bethesda, John speaks of a pool with five porches. This was seen as being nonhistorical and probably symbolic. However, recent archaeological research has indeed revealed the existence of this pool with its five actual porches. Similarly some critics have challenged the authenticity of the words of John the Baptist in the Gospels. It was said that the way he spoke was not found in the Old Testament. Hence they judged it to be nonauthentic. However, the Dead Sea Scrolls, found in 1947, revealed that the vocabulary of John the Baptist was quite similar to that of the Essenes, a religious group about whom little was known until the Qumran scrolls were found. Hence the authenticity of his vocabulary has been substantiated.

Alleged Contradictions in the Bible

But some may say, "This is all well and good; nonetheless is it not true that the Bible often contradicts itself? Does this not then lead to the conclusion that the Bible contains errors?" In answer to this we would point out that it is unfortunate that in our church we seem to have forgotten an excellent book written by the sainted William F. Arndt, professor of New Testament at Concordia Seminary, St. Louis, Mo., entitled *Does the Bible Contradict Itself?* (St. Louis: Concordia Publishing House, 1955; first ed. 1926) In the introduction Dr. Arndt says: "It will have to be granted that if the Scriptures do contain actual discrepancies, they have not in every part been given by divine inspiration. To make contradictory statements means to err, to blunder. The book that contains errors, or blunders, cannot in its entirety come from the great, the all-wise, the perfect God" (p. v). Arndt goes on to point out that we cannot resolve all difficulties. Also in the instance of contradictions in numbers, occasionally we may conclude that there have been errors by the copyists of the Bible. None-theless, in many, many instances we can by careful study demonstrate that apparent contradictions are in fact no con-tradictions at all. I have time for only one example. It is a sig-nificant one since in the Lutheran Church in recent years it has been repeatedly raised by some as an example of an error in the Bible. This is the question of the age of Abraham when he left his homeland. In Gen. 11:26 we read: "When Terah [Abraham's father] had lived seventy years, he became the father of Abram, Nahor, and Haran." In Gen. 11:32 we read that the days of Terah were 205 years and Terah died in Haran. In Gen. 12:4, that Abraham was 75 years old when he de-parted from Haran. In Acts 7:4 we read: "After his father died, God removed him [Abraham] from there into this land in which you are now living." In Arndt's words: "Comparing these four passages, apparently a contradiction looms up. If Terah was seventy years old when Abram was born and lived to be 205 years old, then Abram was 135 years old at the time of his father's death. And if he left Haran only after his father's demise, he must have been a man of at least 135 years when the migration into the Land of Promise was under-taken. That contradicts the statement, Gen. 12:4, that Abram was seventy-five years old when he departed from Haran" (p. 5). However, Arndt continues: "But all this rests on an assumption which is not demanded by the text, namely, on the theory that Abram was the oldest of the sons of Terah and was born when his father was seventy years old" (p. 5). Arndt goes on to point out that while Abraham is mentioned as the first of the three sons, this may be because he was the firstborn, but it may also be because Abraham was the most prominent of the three. If we assume that he was not the oldest but the youngest, then he may have been born when his father was 130 years old. At the time of his father's death Abraham would be 75, thus placing Genesis 12:4 and Acts 7:4 in perfect harmony! We are not always in a position to solve apparent contradictions so handily. Nevertheless we should be aware that a solution may exist, even if we have not been able to find it. Let us avoid, then, the presumptuous conclusion that the Bible may be in error.

Science and the Bible

But, someone may ask, What about science? Wasn't perhaps Bultmann right when he said that the Bible accepts the false world view of the early Jews and is therefore unscientific? Has not science definitely proved that belief in supernatural things, such as miracles, is simply foolishness?

C. S. Lewis, University of Oxford, England, wrote a book entitled *Miracles* (New York: McMillan Co., 1947). He points out that people often labor under the misconception that people in olden times believed in miracles because they didn't know the laws of nature. Very clearly, to Joseph the idea of Mary having a child without a human father was just as great a miracle and just as difficult a thing to believe as it would be for a modern scientist. The scientist knows several things about birth and conception which Joseph did not know. But one thing Joseph did know clearly was that a woman did not conceive a child unless a man was involved. The same thing is true of the wedding at Cana. We know a great deal more about wine and the process of fermentation than did the ancients. Our chemistry is far advanced. Nonetheless, for wine to be formed without fermentation was to them just as great a miracle as it would be for us today. (Today we might note, of course, the additional fact that the miracle involved also the creation of the carbon atom found in the organic compounds in wine, but not in water.)

C. S. Lewis also points out that miracles are by definition and by their nature outside the area where God acts normally in nature. In calling a miracle a miracle, we should not call it a contradiction or a scientific outrage. We merely mean that nature "left to her own resources, could never produce them" (p. 75). It was simply a matter of God acting directly. It is neither scientific or nonscientific to believe in them.

This can be turned around. Lewis also points out that Professor Whitehead asserts that "centuries of belief in a God who combined 'the personal energy of Jehovah' with 'the rationality of a Greek philosopher' first produced that firm expectation of systematic order which rendered possible the birth of modern science. Men became scientific because they expected Law in Nature, and they expected Law in Nature because they believed in a Legislator" (pp. 127 – 28). This may have died down in many modern scientists, but it remains a historical fact. The very existence of miracles reminds us that God normally does not act that way, but in a more systematic way.

There are many, many Christians who are scientists and also humble believers in God in Christ and who have been brought to that faith by the Holy Scriptures. For example, Dr. Donald S. Kerlee, American physicist, states: "A Christian view of science recognizes the excellence of science in its description of the physical world. Beyond the scope of science, however, the Christian recognizes parameters of experience not measured by units of length, mass, or time, nor easily expressed in units derived therefrom. . . . A Christian view of science admits the revelation of God in nature through his creation, as well as through special revelation, the holy Scriptures." [14] A distinguished British biochemist, Malcolm

Dixon, reports: "For over forty years I have been engaged in scientific research and teaching at the advanced level in Cambridge University, and I have found no reason to think that there is any incompatibility between science and Christianity. Many of the greatest scientists have been Christian believers, and I should judge that there is now in this country about the same proportion of such believers among scientists as among non-scientists." (Ibid.)

But perhaps someone will be thinking, yes, this may be true concerning accepting Christianity and the Bible in general, but if I want to hold to a strict doctrine of creation as told in Genesis, will I not as a creationist find all scientists believing in evolution instead? I will come back to this later in the last part of the essay. However, at this time I think we ought to deal with the question as to whether or not every competent scientist is an evolutionist. Of course, we must face the fact that one does not decide truth by voting or by counting noses. Nonetheless this disturbing claim has been made quite often and we ought to lay this ghost to rest. The fact of the matter is that one frequently encounters competent scientists who are believers in creation and who reject evolution. The Creation Research Society numbers in its membership several hundred scientists thoroughly committed to creation. One finds such men in the great universities and in industry. They reject evolution not only because of their religious beliefs, but because they see so much scientific evidence that speaks against the theory. They are undoubtedly not in the majority, but they do exist in considerable numbers. Moreover, their existence demonstrates the error of the propaganda statement of some evolutionists that all competent scientists accept the theory.

The fact of the matter is that when we deal with the past we are in a field where Scripture itself has told us very little and we ought not to attempt to make Scripture say more than the Holy Spirit has. We are also, however, working in a field where science is likewise handicapped by a lack of information. That scientific theories concerning the origin of the universe and of life are in this speculative category can easily be illustrated. It is recognized by many scientists who on occasion warn their colleagues about this. Moreover, as science makes progress, what often seemed to have been rather firmly established theories have to be abandoned. This is not to the discredit but to the credit of science. However, it does serve to warn us against becoming overly impressed in areas where science is handicapped in its approach.

Such an area is the question of life coming into existence without God having created it. This so-called evolution of life has received a great deal of attention recently. Some years ago two chemists, Drs. Miller and Urey, radiated a mixture of methane gas, ammonia, and water with an electrical discharge and ultraviolet light. The result was the formation of several complex organic compounds. Miller, Urey, and others promptly hailed this as evidence that living forms could conceivably have developed out of very elementary gases. Recently this theory was given a severe setback when a number of chemists studied organic compounds trapped in carbon-containing meteorites.[15] It was assumed that these meteorites contained traces of the primordial gases which would have been trapped from a so-called primitive gas phase at the time of the formation of the earth. The meteorites were found to contain a collection of gas including hydrogen, methane, carbon monoxide, carbon dioxide, nitrogen oxide, nitrogen, sulphur dioxide, and carbon disulphide, plus a few organic compounds such as benzene and anthracene. However, ammonia, an essential ingredient for the Miller-Urey process, was *not* detected. The researchers concluded that it now will be necessary to find some other type of process in the solar nebula to explain the prebiological organic matter on earth and that the Miller-Urey reactions apparently have no foundation.

Edwin C. Webb, professor of biochemistry at the University of Queensland, and Malcolm Dixon of Cambridge analyzed the difficulty in conceiving of enzymes coming into existence in an evolutionary process. Their analysis is too technical for us to include in this essay, but they concluded: "Thus the whole subject of the origin of enzymes, like that of the origin of life, which is essentially the same thing, bristles with difficulties. We may surely say of the advent of enzymes, as Hopkins said of the advent of life, that it was 'the most improbable and the most significant event in the history of the Universe.'" [16]

While evolutionary chemists are very enthusiastic about the possibility of life having formed itself, others are extremely skeptical and point out that the probability is all against it. This point was made quite effectively in a symposium on the origin of life, where one of the papers was entitled "The Folly of Probability." The author, Peter T. Mora, discusses the extremely difficult assumptions which are required to postulate the evolution of living forms, their preservation, and propagation. He points out that difficulties are sometimes evaded by propagandists for the theory by the use of what he calls "escape clauses." He says: "A further aspect I should like to discuss is what I call the practice of infinite escape clauses. I believe we developed this practice to avoid facing the conclusion that the probability of a self-reproducing state is zero. This is what we must conclude from classical quantum mechanical principles. . . . These escape clauses postulate an almost infinite amount of time and an almost infinite amount of material (monomers), so that even the most unlikely event could have happened. This is to invoke probability and statistical considerations when such considerations are meaningless. When for practical purposes the condition of infinite time and matter has to be invoked, the concept of probability is annulled. By such logic we can prove anything, such as that no matter how complex, everything will repeat itself, exactly and innumerably." [17]

It is apparent that here is one scientist who is tired of men evading the improbability of life forming itself being minimized by the use of "escape clauses," by invoking the help of billions of years. He indicates that when these difficulties are admitted, science is also reduced to faith in a dogma.

The Bible Speaks for Itself

But it is important that we realize that we do not regard the Holy Scriptures to be true and reliable in all respects simply because we are convinced that they have not been disproved or because we can show that science in its own area is fallible. The sole and only reason we believe that the Holy Scriptures are what they claim to be is because we are convinced of this by God's Holy Spirit, working through these selfsame Scriptures. Christ tells us we are to "search the Scriptures, for in them ye think ye have eternal life; and they are they which testify of Me" (John 5:39). On the road to Emmaus, on Easter evening, Christ does not immediately reveal Himself as the risen Savior to the disciples. But rather He says, "O foolish men, and slow of heart to believe all that the prophets have spoken! Was it not necessary that the Christ should suffer these things and enter into His glory? And beginning with Moses and all the prophets He interpreted to them in all the Scriptures the things concerning Himself" (Luke 24:25-27). Christ leaves no doubt here that they should have expected His resurrection as well as His suffering on the basis of what the Old Testament told them. This is characteristic of His regard of the Old Testament and can be repeated again and again in numerous examples found in the Gospels.

Likewise the Gospel writers again and again speak of the fulfillment of prophecy. They say that Christ experienced this or that or did this or that "that it might be fulfilled" which was written in the Scriptures. Matthew begins it by saying, "All of this took place to fulfill what the Lord had spoken by the prophet, 'Behold, a virgin shall conceive and bear a son and His name shall be called Emmanuel' " (Matt. 1:22-23). Again and again he comes back to this theme. He records that Jesus in the very hour of His capture in the Garden of Gethsemane says: "Have you come out as against a robber, with swords and clubs to capture Me? Day after day I sat in the temple teaching, and you did not seize Me. But all this has taken place that the Scriptures of the prophets might be fulfilled." (Matt. 26:55-56)

Again and again we find this reflected in the Book of Acts, coupled with the very significant development that now the apostles are also testifying to the things which they have seen and heard and which the Holy Spirit has led them to utter. In the days after Christ's resurrection Peter stood up and reminded the brethren concerning the fate of Judas, that it was that "which the Holy Spirit spoke beforehand by the mouth of David" (Acts 1:16). And then they selected Matthias as the replacement for Judas. The requirement for this replacement was that he had to be one who had accompanied the apostles "during all the time that the Lord Jesus went in and out among us, beginning from the baptism of John until the day when He was taken up from us—one of these men must become with us a witness to His resurrection" (Acts 1:21-22). The things concerning Christ's ministry are not things that were added by the church later. They are eyewitness accounts of the apostles themselves. This alone, we should note, is one of the strong arguments against form criticism, which often attributes some of these accounts to later additions by the ecclesiastical community.

In the 18th chapter of Acts, Apollos is said to have been a mighty force for Christianity, "for he powerfully confuted the Jews in public, showing by the Scriptures that the Christ was Jesus" (Acts 18:28). When Paul speaks before the Roman governor Felix, he says: "I worship the God of our fathers, believing everything laid down by the Law or written in the Prophets" (Acts 24:14). Paul had no hesitancy in indicating that his faith led him to accept every last word of the Holy Scriptures.

Instances like these could be repeated again and again. Moreover, we recall that Christ assured His apostles that they in turn would be led by the Spirit and influenced by the Comforter whom He would send. This applied also to Paul when he was called by Christ to be His apostle. Paul is quite definite about the source of his Gospel. He tells the Galatians: "For I would have you know, brethren, that the Gospel which was preached by me is not man's gospel. For I did not receive it from man, nor was I taught it, but it came through a revelation of Jesus Christ" (Gal. 1:11-12). He is confident of the validity of his teaching and that it is guided by the Spirit. Thus he tells the Corinthians: "We impart this in words not taught by human wisdom but taught by the Spirit, interpreting spiritual truths to those who possess the Spirit" (1 Cor. 2:13). The writer to the Hebrews takes away any thought anyone might have that this is only an intellectual process when he says: "The Word of God is living and active, sharper than any two-edged sword, piercing to the division of soul and spirit, of joints and marrow, and discerning the thoughts and intentions of the heart." (Heb. 4:12)

Peter, in his letters, speaks of the prophets of old. He indicates beyond any doubt the revelation by the Spirit when he says: "The prophets who prophesied of the grace that was to be yours searched and inquired about this salvation; they inquired what person or time was indicated by the Spirit of Christ within them when predicting the sufferings of Christ and the subsequent glory. It was revealed to them that they were serving not themselves but you, in the things which have now been announced to you by those who preach the good news for you through the Holy Spirit sent from heaven, things into which angels long to look" (1 Peter 1:10-12). The same apostle in his second letter points out that "no prophecy ever came by the impulse of man, but men moved by the Holy Spirit spoke from God" (2 Peter 1:21). And, of course, there is that famous passage in which Paul tells Timothy that he has been well trained, has not been deceived, and that "from childhood you have been acquainted with the sacred writings which are able to instruct you for salvation through faith in Christ Jesus. All Scripture is inspired by God and profitable for teaching, for reproof, for correction, and for training in righteousness, that the man of God may be complete, equipped for every good work." (2 Tim. 3:15-17)

Going back to Peter, we note with interest that in his last letter he speaks of Paul writing to them according to the wisdom given to him and says that there are things in Paul's writings which are hard to understand, which "the ignorant and unstable twist to their own destruction, as they do the other Scriptures." (2 Peter 3:16)

These passages in Old and New Testament make it clear that the holy writers regarded themselves as inspired by the Holy Spirit not only in connection with things of which they were eyewitnesses or, as Luke indicates in his preface, where they were able to check with eyewitnesses, but in matters where the Spirit spoke to them directly in terms of revelation.

Inerrancy of the Bible

Luther says, "Scripture . . . has never erred" (*LW*, 32, 11). He also says, "It is impossible that Scripture should contradict itself" (St. L. Ed., IX, 356). In the Large Catechism he writes, "My neighbor and I—in short all men—may err and deceive, but God's Word cannot err."

Examples of this kind could be multiplied from the history of the church. Men have constantly said that, because of the nature of inspiration, because of the nature of God's Word, because of the way it is treated in Old and New Testament by the prophets and apostles, by Christ Himself, it is impossible to escape the concept of the inerrancy of the Bible. In this connection it is instructive to quote a section from an article by Robert Preus of Concordia Seminary, St. Louis.

> The nature of inerrancy is essentially twofold: Scripture does not lie or deceive, and Scripture does not err or make mistakes in any affirmation it makes. . . . In other words, the holy writers, moved by the Spirit of God, infallibly achieve the intent of their writing. . . . This is what is meant when we say that Scripture is a *reliable witness* to the words and deeds of God. Of His people God demands in the second and eighth commandments that they tell the truth; of His prophets and apostles, that they do not lie. God will not countenance lying and prevarication (Prov. 14:5; 19:22; Ps. 63:11; Jer. 23:25 ff.; Zeph. 3:13; Acts 5:3; 1 John 2:21, 27). And God Himself will not lie or deceive (Prov. 30:6-7; Num. 23:19; Ps. 89:35; Heb. 6:18). In His written Word He will not break or suspend that standard of truth which He demands of His children. Thus we hear frequently from God's inspired witnesses the claim that they do not deceive, that they are not mistaken, that they tell the truth (Rom. 9:1; 2 Cor. 11:31; Gal. 1:20; 1 Tim. 2:7). The whole impact of entire books of the Bible depends on the authoritative and faithful witness of the writer. (John 21:24; 1 John 1:1-5a; 2 Peter 1:15-18)

Pertinent to what was just said is the following. The truth of the sacred Scriptures must be determined from the sense which is intended (in verse, pericope, book) by the author. This sense in turn must be determined according to sound hermeneutical rules.

It is obvious that such a position on the nature of Biblical inerrancy is predicated on a correspondence idea of truth which in part means this: Declarative statements (at least in those Biblical genres, or literary forms, which purport to be dealing with fact or history) of Scripture are, according to their intention, true in that they correspond to what has taken place (for example, historical statements), to what obtains (for example, theological affirmations and other affirmations concerning fact), or to what will take place (for example, predictive prophecy). It really ought to go without saying that . . . Scripture, like all cognitive discourse, operates under the rubrics of a correspondence idea of truth. (See John 8:46; Eph. 4:25; 1 Kings 8:26; 22:16, 22 ff.; Gen. 42:16, 20; Deut. 18:22; Ps. 119:163; Dan. 2:9; Prov. 14:25; Zech. 8:16; John 5:21-32 ff.; Acts 24:8, 11; 1 Tim. 1:15; note too, the forensic picture which haunts all of Scripture—for example, such concepts as witness, testimony, judge, the Eighth Commandment, etc.; John 21:24.)

To speak of inerrancy of purpose (that God achieves His purpose in Scripture) or of Christological inerrancy of Scripture is indeed relevant to the general question of inerrancy, but may at the same time be misleading if such a construct is understood as constituting the nature of inerrancy—for then we might speak of the inerrancy of Luther's Small Catechism or of a hymn by Paul Gerhardt, since they successfully achieve their purpose.[18]

It is safe to say that nowhere in Scripture does one find any statement which limits the inerrancy of Scripture. The limits which are sometimes placed on the inerrancy of Scripture by theologians today as in past times are based on external arguments and rationalizations. If only we could in simple faith continue to accept Scripture for what it claims to be, in its totality the Word of God. When men attempt to tamper with Scripture or subtract from it in one way or another, all too often the result has been an utter bankruptcy of theology. As we have seen earlier, the unwillingness to admit the verbal inspiration of Scripture and to equate it with the Word of God has sometimes reduced hermeneutics to a mystical process which to scientists is far more unscientific than to take the first and simple step of believing that God is able and willing to speak to His people through His prophets and apostles.

Theistic Evolution

Genesis 1 and 2

I would like to go into some detail concerning the question of theistic evolution. This is important because it is a live issue in our church and because it is so closely related to the questions we have been talking about — inspiration and the methods of interpreting the Word of God. For there are some who claim that we no longer can teach the 6-day creation as taught in Genesis because, they feel, this has been conclusively disproved by modern science, while evolution has been thoroughly proved. They feel that the opening chapters of Genesis, going all the way through the 11th chapter, are to be regarded as a mythological and really a factually erroneous account of the beginnings. They feel that we ought to conclude from these chapters nothing more than that God somehow was behind the origin of the universe, the world, and man, and that man somehow fell short and disappointed God. They hold that it is not intended to teach us any facts concerning the beginning. They believe that if it is not outright mythology, then it is perhaps poetic and figurative language which is not intended to provide us with any information other than the general idea that God is behind nature.

Is this true? Is it possible for us, as faithful interpreters of Scripture and believers in God's Word, to accept theistic evolution? If we do so, what are the consequences, if any? Have we perhaps, out of a stubborn conservative spirit, been dragging our feet when we should have gone along with evolution? There are many who feel that our insistence on creation as opposed to evolution imposes an intellectual obstacle to the faith of young people in today's scientific age. Perhaps this will be a good topic to use as a sort of case history in which some of the things we have been talking about can be applied in a definite situation.

Let us begin with a few simple definitions. By "evolution" we mean the complete theory of evolution from the so-called first gaseous plasma, which is said to have preceded the formation of the elements, down to man. By "theistic evolution" we mean that, instead of this process being governed by the rules of chance and natural selection, as held by evolutionists, it is directed by God.

By "creation" we mean that God originally created certain "kinds" in the beginning of the world's history. We are not told specifically what are included in the "kinds," with the exception of man, who is mentioned on the sixth day. The use of the term "kind" in Leviticus 11, however, makes quite clear that it is a term larger than species, perhaps large enough in some instances to include a family or order. It is not possible precisely to define the exact limits of the category "kind" as used in Genesis 1. That there are limits is clear in the text from the constant repetition of the phrase that things reproduce "after their kind." This does not rule out variation or even the possibility of the origin of new species or new genera. It would rule out the production of new "kinds." Thus it would allow for the variety which is shown in the fossil record, but it would rule out the production of a new kind such as man from a lower form of life.

Another preliminary item deals with the question of "time." Actually the age of the earth does not lie at the heart of the problem. A great age for the earth is a vital requirement for the evolutionist; it is much less important for the creationist. The evolutionist needs it for new forms to develop. The creationist does not.

I do not have the time to go into an extensive treatment of the word *yom,* which is translated "day" in Genesis 1. I cannot pass it by, however, without a few general remarks. These considerations may be listed as follows.

a. We do not understand either theologically or scientifically the essence of "time."

b. We are dealing with an account of the origin of all things in which "time" as well as "space" is in the process of being created. This alone may rule out any common-sense notions or scientific notions we have of "time" today.

c. I would agree with Edward Young, who says: "The six days are to be understood in a chronological sense, that is, one day following another in succession. This fact is emphasized in that the days are designated, one, two, three, etc." [19]

d. The creation days are best designated as just that — *creation days.*

e. The text does not give us the length of the days. The constant repetition of the formula "evening and morning," which is associated in verse 3 with light and darkness, points forcibly, however, to a day governed by a succession of light and darkness.

Nevertheless, Oesch has pointed out that "the Christian church has nowhere dogmatized the present measurement of time (24 hours) for these days. For that purpose the anomalies of the first and seventh days are simply too great." [20] Oesch asserts that there is a question whether or not the time of the Spirit sweeping over the "deep" is to be included in the first day (p. 75, n. 31). Originally there was darkness. Then God created light. This light is called "day." Then comes evening and then comes morning — "first day." There is a succession of darkness and light followed by darkness and light, indicating that the first day may follow the activity of the Spirit over the deep. Oesch also recognizes, as do other commentators, that the first three days were not solar days such as we now have, inasmuch as the sun, moon, and stars had not yet been made (ibid.). Some, however, think that the activity of the fourth day was a clearing up of the atmosphere and revealing the fact that these heavenly bodies had been placed there previously.

The sainted George V. Schick and Walter A. Maier, professors of Hebrew at Concordia Seminary, St. Louis, consistently held that the text supported the idea of an ordinary day, particularly in view of Ex. 20:8-11, where the Sabbath rule is established. The modern Interpreter's Bible agrees and states: "There can be no question but that by 'day' the author meant just what we mean — the time required for one revolution of the earth on its axis. Had he meant an aeon he would certainly, in view of his fondness for great numbers, have stated the number of millenniums each period embraced." [21]

The attempt to stretch the days out to long periods of time generally is unsuccessful in bringing about the desired harmonization of Genesis with geology.

One would like to dwell on this intriguing topic, but it does not get us to the heart of the problem. The real question is, Can we accept the evolution of man from a lower form of life?

We cannot make any progress in answering the question until we decide whether or not Genesis is patently unscientific. By this I do not mean to deal with the question of whether or not it is a scientific textbook. This red herring ought to be buried permanently. The question rather is, Does it contain information which is correct in substance? Bernard Ramm said it well when he stated that "religion is not pure spirit, pure eternal fact. The evangelical faith has doctrines which directly pertain to the world of fact. The verse which opens the canon of Sacred Scripture refers to Nature, namely, its creation by Almighty God. The Incarnation and Resurrection are in the stream of history." [22]

There are some who attempt to persuade us that the Bible contains the world view of the ancient Jews, which might be described somewhat as follows: "In the Scripture the flat earth is founded on an underlying sea; it is stationary; the heavens are like an upturned bowl or canopy above it; the circumference of this vault rests on pillars; the sun, moon, and stars move within this firmament of special purpose to illumine man; there is a sea above the sky, 'the waters which were above the heavens,' and through the 'windows of heaven' the rain comes down; within the earth is Sheol, where dwell the shadowy dead; this whole cosmic system is suspended over vacancy; and it was all made in six days with a morning and an evening a short and measurable time before." [23]

Statements like this are repeated so often that we finally begin to believe them even though they are not based on Scripture's teaching. Carl Gaenssle in the October 1952 *Concordia Theological Monthly* marshals Biblical evidence to show that Scripture does not teach such a cosmology.

Gaenssle cites passages such as Is. 40:22; Ps. 104:2; and Is. 34:4, in which the heavens are referred to as being stretched out like a curtain, like a tent, and as being due to be rolled up at the end of time like a scroll. Gaenssle asks: "Can anyone with these texts before him seriously and honestly believe that the writers of these words entertained the crude and inept notion of a metallic canopy above their heads?" [24] With reference to the seas he concludes: "Consequently, when the earth is said to be founded on the seas and spread out upon the waters, there is no reason to assume that the Psalmist is singing of an invisible ocean on which the earth rests or is spread out, but only of earthly waters on which the earth touches and over which it is elevated" (p. 747). Ramm quotes Gaenssle with reference to the Hebrew word *tehom:* "The upper, terrestrial ocean satisfies all requirements, and it lies below or beneath in the same sense as the Dead Sea lies under Mount Pisgah and the land of Moab" (Gaenssle, p. 749). Ramm also adds that the pillars of the earth mentioned in Job 9:6 are the rocks which bear up the surface of the earth.

It is interesting that the English physicist Frederick A. Filby takes the same position regarding the word for the atmosphere which is actually mistranslated as "firmament." He says:

> The original idea behind the Hebrew word *raqia* (firmament) seems to be the process of beating or stamping out. In the development of language this has led to two distinct meanings. If clay in a mould is stamped on it will become compressed — firmer — more solid. . . . But the word *raqia* was connected with a second and much commoner conception. If gold or silver was beaten or stamped out it became very thin. The ancients were in fact very good at this process and specimens of their work show that they used gold leaf down to 1/5000 of an inch think. The word thus

> acquired the meanings of expanse and of thinness and
> we find this borne out in related expressions such as
> the word *raq* used for Pharaoh's "thin" kine and *raqiq*
> used for "wafers." [25]

Filby goes on to point out that this description of the expanse beyond the earth, of the atmosphere and outer space beyond, is really a very accurate one.

We ought not pass this point without remembering that not so many years ago the concept of *creatio ex nihilo* (creation out of nothing) was regarded as being most unscientific. This was before the discovery that energy and matter are convertible. I am not attempting to demonstrate that the Bible can be used as any kind of a scientific textbook. I am saying, however, that where we have been patient enough to study it thoroughly, and also from time to time to progress in our concept of nature, we have not found the Bible wanting. We need more patience and ought not fall into the snare of declaring the Bible to be in error because we cannot solve all the difficulties that presently face us.

In asking whether or not theistic evolution may be found in the text, we must come to grips with the question as to what kind of literature we have in Genesis 1. Unless we decide the kind of literature we are dealing with, we cannot perform good exegesis. If it is historical prose, that is one thing. If it is poetry or myth or saga or symphony, that is quite another.

In an unpublished paper delivered to the Rock Symposium, a subcommittee of the Missouri Synod's Committee on Scholarly Research, Robert Preus of Concordia Seminary, St. Louis, indicated that roughly speaking all interpretations of Genesis fall into two general classifications. First of all there is approach A. "This approach makes the account figurative, a-historical or supra-historical, and ultimately non-descriptive. The genre of the story will be called myth, poem, parable, epic, saga, depending upon the predilection of the exegete." [26] Thus the account will be taken as:

a. a demythologized poem sung to the glory of the creator God.

b. an aetiological saga, offering an explanation of questions which must have puzzled the Israelites in the 10th century B. C.

c. a cosmology, like many other epic and legendary cosmologies of the day, but purified of theogony, theomachy, and other unworthy elements.

d. "inspired" Hebrew borrowing from the sacred writings and legends of near-neighbor cultures.

e. a similar reworking of ancient Hebrew myths into one organic account, didactic in nature.

These approaches vary considerably. They are alike, however, in having a strong emphasis on the long development of the creation story and a general eliminating of the possibility that Moses received a divine revelation of what really did take place at creation. They also stress the polemical nature of the account, namely that it is against polytheism and false cosmologies. Parenthetically, the essayist would add at this point that there certainly is a polemical note in Genesis 1. However, these various approaches go on to discount the idea that the Genesis account could possibly be descriptive of what actually happened.

Preus points out that there is another approach, namely approach B. "This approach accepts Genesis 1 as a chronological account of something that actually happened in creation. Genesis 1 and 2 offer us correct and satisfactory *information* concerning prehistoric times and *Urgeschichte*" (p. 7). Leupold in his *Exposition of Genesis* states that the account "goes back beyond the reach of available historical sources and offers not mythical suppositions, not poetical

103

fancies, not vague suggestions, but a positive record of things as they actually transpired and, at the same time, of matters of infinite moment for all mankind." [27]

Preus goes on to say that such an understanding of Genesis 1 and 2 is basic to a full understanding of our doctrine of sin and redemption (Law and Gospel). "This interpretation insists that the Biblical account is utterly superior to the other cosmogonies of the day and is therefore not a derivative of any of them, although Moses may have been aware of these accounts and used aspects of them. Such an approach in no way implies that metaphors, anthropomorphisms, and other figures of speech are not employed, e. g., God speaks, walks in the garden. . . . But in none of these cases may we say that God did nothing. For instance, when God spoke, something happened; this means He did speak." [28]

Preus goes on to indicate that position B has basic theological concerns. "It insists that the Genesis account agree with the rest of Scripture on the themes mentioned (e. g., Romans 5). Thus, theologically one must insist upon a created universe with a transcendent God (against all forms of pantheism and naturalism), a created human man and woman (against evolutionism and polygenesis), a man created in a state of perfection, and an actual, historical fall (against all mythological explanations of man's present sinful condition). This is interpreting Genesis 1 and 2 in terms of Law and Gospel." (P. 9)

Still further complicating the picture is the insistence of many interpreters, including some who assert that they hold to verbal inspiration, that Genesis 2 actually contains a separate and conflicting report from Genesis 1. It is said that Genesis 1 represents the writing of the priestly writer, who uses the word *Elohim* for God, whereas Gen. 2:4b through 2:24 is an account of the writer designated as J, who uses the word *Yahweh* or Jehovah. This immediately plunges us into a consideration of the documentary hypothesis with all of its ramifications. For the purposes of our essay, I am assuming that there is no conflict in Scripture and that we do not have conflicting elements standing side by side. I am also assuming the correctness of scholars such as Walter A. Maier and George V. Schick, both of them holding doctorates in Hebrew, who rejected the documentary hypothesis. They are not alone in that, however. In a recent publication from Hebrew University in Jerusalem, M. H. Segal says: "The preceding pages have made it clear why we must reject the Documentary Theory as an explanation of the composition of the Pentateuch. The Theory is complicated, artificial and anomalous. It is based on unproved assumptions. It uses unreliable criteria for the separation of the text into component documents." [29]

Segal goes on to examine the alleged duplications of several accounts which are to be found in Genesis and declares:

> A careful examination of these narratives will show that the alleged duplication is either only apparent or based upon an incorrect exegesis. Thus it is said that [Gen.] ii, 4ff. gives another story of the Creation belonging to the J document as distinguished from the preceding story in i-ii, 3 which is assigned to the P document. But ii, 4ff. cannot be like i, 1-ii, 3 an account of the creation of the world, since it says nothing of the creation of the firmament, the seas, the luminaries and other essential elements of the world. The truth is that ii, 4ff. is an integral part of the story of man's sin and punishment. Its purpose is to describe the environment of man before his sin, the garden and its plants and its animals, and the detailed creation of the woman. The description differs indeed in its style and viewpoint and in some details from the story

in i, 1-ii, 3 but this is not sufficient to prove a different
author (pp. 100—101).

This is in harmony with the traditional position that in Genesis
2 we have a zooming in of the lens of revelation to tell us
what happened in the Garden of Eden as distinct from the
events at large in the universe and on the planet earth.

But this still leaves unanswered the question as to
whether or not the accounts in Genesis 1 and 2 are in fact
historical. In support of taking the Genesis 1 and 2 account
as a recording of what did in fact take place we note the
following supporting evidence.

First, the form as we have it is essentially a straight-
forward prose account. While it contains certain lofty concepts
and figures of speech such as anthropomorphisms, there is
no indication that it is anything but a factual account. We do
not think of it as history in the sense that it is verifiable history,
as for example the history of the Civil War, where one may go
back and do research in terms of establishing a certain point
of interest. It is history which must have been based on
revelation, but history nonetheless, in the sense that it is an
account of what actually did happen. It is interesting that the
Jewish scholar E. A. Speiser in his commentary in the Anchor
Bible translation of Genesis appears to support this assertion.
He says:

> What we have here is not primarily a description of
> events or a reflection of a unique experience. Rather,
> we are given the barest statement of a sequence of facts
> resulting from the fiat of the supreme and absolute
> master of the universe. . . . The ultimate objective was
> to set forth, in a manner that must not presume in any
> way to edit the achievement of the Creator—by the
> slightest injection of sentiment or personality—not

a theory but a credo, a credo untinged by the least hint of speculation. . . . Genesis i-xi in general, and the first section in particular, are a broad introduction to the history which commences with Abraham. The practice of tracing history back to antediluvian times is at least as old as the Sumerian king list.[30]

The concept that Genesis is indeed historical is supported by the genealogical list in Genesis 5, where we are told of the birth of Seth, who in turn was the father of Enoch, who was the father of Cainan, etc., until we come to Noah. The same list occurs in Luke 3, and one cannot avoid the conclusion that there is a reference here to real people. Certainly there is no parallel for this kind of procedure in the poetic literature of the Old Testament.

Another consideration is the phrase in chapter 2, verse 4: "These are the generations: of the heavens and the earth when they were created." A similar formula is found in Gen. 5:1, where it says: "This is the book of the generations of Adam"; 6:9 ("These are the generations of Noah"); 10:1; 11:10, 27; 25:12, 19; 36:1, 9; and 37:2. Oesch points out that this formula stands as a superscription over a historical listing which is to follow (p. 72). Since it stands over the account of Adam and the special creation of Eve in the same manner that it stands over other historical listings, it would point to Genesis 2 as being historically factual.

Against these indications of the historical nature of Genesis 1 and 2 several approaches have been set forth in the interest of viewing Genesis 1 and 2 as accounts which are polemical against heathen concepts and which teach the sovereignty of God, the goodness of God, etc., but which teach nothing concerning the so-called "how of creation." It has been said that the chief purpose of Genesis is to serve as praise and that it is one of several portraits of creation given in the Bible. Other portraits are Psalm 104, Proverbs 8, and Job 38 and 39. The implication is that all of these accounts are ways in which the Jews praised God the Creator. The basic weakness of this approach lies in the presupposition that because there are psalms of praise to the Creator in the Bible, the Genesis account must by virtue of that very fact be one of these. It really begs the question by asserting what is to be proved. An examination of Psalm 104 and a comparison of this psalm with the Genesis 1 and 2 account reveals a vast difference between them. First of all, the psalm account has the characteristic Hebrew parallelism of phrases and sentences, which is the form of Hebrew poetry. Genesis does not have this. Furthermore, Psalm 104 starts out with the words: "Bless the Lord, O my soul! O Lord my God, Thou art very great!" It thus clearly indicates that it is a hymn of blessing. This is quite different from the beginning of Genesis, which says: "In the beginning God created." One labels itself as a hymn of praise, the other does not.

Furthermore, it is incorrect to label accounts such as Psalm 104 as creation accounts. Psalm 104 makes no reference to the creation of animals and no reference to the creation of man. Another account which is sometimes mentioned is Proverbs 8. Here is no mention made of sun, moon, and stars or of man or woman. These same arguments apply to Job 38 – 39. These are undoubtedly references to the creation account. But they are built on the supposition that everyone knows the account of Genesis 1 and 2, and these are reflections on various phases of the creative activity. This in no way indicates that the Genesis account is of the same nature as the poetic reflections thereon. It is much the same fallacy as to say that Genesis 1 and 2 cannot be factual because the last book in the Bible is Revelation and this is apocalyptic in nature. There is no logical or theological basis for assertions of this kind.

More to the point is the endeavor of those individuals who point out that there are certain figurative expressions in Genesis. Reference is made to the fact that God is described as speaking, that He breathes into man's nostrils, that He molds man from the dust of the earth, etc. The argumentation is that these anthropomorphic elements lead us to believe that we are dealing with an extended figurative expression.

An examination of the use of anthropomorphisms in the Bible leads to the conclusion that their presence in an account does not ipso facto render it a figurative or poetic account. For example, in Gen. 19:29 we read: "It came to pass, when God destroyed the cities of the plain, that God *remembered* Abraham." The fact that the anthropomorphic expression "remembered" is used does not take away from the historical account that the cities were actually destroyed. In Ex. 3:8 God says: "I have come down to deliver them out of the hand of the Egyptians." Again the fact that God is spoken of as coming down does not mean that there was no deliverance out of the bondage in Egypt. Similarly Christ in Luke 11:20 says: "It is by the finger of God that I cast out demons." The reference to the finger of God would certainly not mean that the casting out of demons is something which did not actually take place. We would conclude that it takes something more than the presence of an anthropomorphism to render an account nonprose and nonfactual.

Young also points out that, while there are anthropomorphic terms in Genesis 2, they are rather limited. He adds: "The words 'and God breathed,' may be termed anthropomorphic, but that is the extent to which the term is employed. The man was real, the dust was real, the ground was real, as was also the breath of life. To these elements of the verse the term anthropomorphism cannot be legitimately applied." [31]

Another point made is that the numbers 7 and 10 occur

rather strikingly in the Genesis account and that the activity of the first three days respectively can be connected with the activity of the last three days respectively. For example, on the first day light was created, and on the corresponding fourth day of the second triad the heavenly bodies were placed in the sky. It is argued that this formal relationship indicates a type of literature which is structured so as to present a story which might easily be memorized. It is concluded that therefore the events recorded are not chronologically narrated or even correspond in any way specifically to what may or may not have happened.

In reply, we would note the following. The fact that there may be a formally structured system in the account may not indicate at all that the account is artificial. It may merely point to an orderly procedure on the part of God. Frederick A. Filby, professor of physics at the University of London, points out that mathematical patterns are common in nature. He mentions the structures of molecules, the lattices of chemical crystals, the arrangement of leaves on the stems of trees, etc. And then he adds: "It is but one step further to realize that the Mathematical Mind that designed the universe has revealed Itself through the pattern of words of Genesis 1. (P. 19)

The same answer might be given to those who say that the reason for the seven days of creation is to explain why the Jews had to rest on the Sabbath Day. This approach assumes that the story is written to justify the law rather than that the law reflects the actual order of creation. It is significant that the six periods of activity occur rather commonly in many of the creation myths of other peoples. It seems to point back to a very early establishment of six as a significant number. The late Prof. G. C. Aalders of the Free University of Amsterdam has said: "In Exodus 20:11 the activity of God is presented to man as a pattern, and this fact presupposes that there was a reality in the activity of God which man is to follow.

How could man be held accountable for working six days if God himself had not actually worked for six days?" [32]

Concerning the scheme of the first three days forming a triad which corresponds to the last three days which form a corresponding triad, with day 1 corresponding to day 4, day 2 to day 5, and day 3 to day 6, it may be observed that this scheme does not hold up on thorough analysis. For example, the light bearers are placed in the firmament on day 4. Day 4 is supposed to correspond to day 1, on which light is created. That is all right. However, they are placed in the firmament on day 4, but the firmament was not made until day 2 and actually should correspond to activities on day 5. Thus the parallelism is imperfect in that day 4 refers to things made on both day 1 and day 2. Another example is the fact that the fish were commanded to swim in the seas on day 5 but the seas were not made until the third day, which corresponds in the supposed scheme of parallelism to the sixth day instead of the fifth day. There are other points in the account which indicate the same lack of parallelism. In other words, while there is a certain general framework, it is not a stilted, artificial framework which might lead us to believe that the events were arranged in nonchronological order. Moreover, it is to be noted that even within the framework hypothesis there is preserved a certain amount of chronology because the events follow in terms of day 1, 2, and 3 and days 4, 5, and 6.

It might be further noted that the arrangement of items in a specific framework does not thereby invalidate these being references to actual facts. A classic example is the genealogy of Christ in the Gospel of Matthew, tracing Christ back to Abraham. The genealogy is arranged into 14 generations from Abraham to David, 14 from David to the deportation to Babylon, and 14 from the deportation to Babylon to Christ. The framework is such that the actual genealogy as found in 1 Chronicles is abridged by the omission of four names so as to fit the 14-14-14 scheme. Nonetheless it serves the purpose of showing that Christ was a descendant of Abraham according to His legal genealogy, which is given here. No one would say that the framework which is used here means that the individuals in the list were not real individuals. The existence of some framework does not justify us in concluding that the events which are recorded may not be factual events. Some scholars also claim that John's Gospel is arranged on the basis of seven days.

Thus it would appear that the position that the account in Genesis 1 and 2 is historical in the sense of providing pre-history and referring to actual events may still be maintained. There is no compelling reason in Scripture for deviating from what is the manifestly first impression one reaches when he examines the text.

Let us go on to an examination of specific words and phrases in Genesis 1 and 2 to see if they lend themselves to theistic evolution. It has been held that the expression in Gen. 1:11: "Let the earth put forth vegetation, plants yielding seed, and fruit trees" and the expression in verse 20: "Let the waters bring forth swarms of living creatures, and let birds fly above the earth across the firmament of the heavens" is indicative of evolution. It is said to refer to a process of development rather than to a fiat creation in response to God's word. However, if Moses were describing an evolutionary process, one would expect it to have been phrased differently—that out of the earth and seas came a simpler form of life, which in turn produced a higher form of life. It is probably best to conclude as does Norman Habel in a series of unpublished theses that "no hidden clue of evolution can be legitimately extracted from this passage." It is more likely that what is discussed here is the fact that once these things sprang forth in response to God's creative word, the process of God's providence took over. This is parallel to man being told to fill the earth and subdue it, a process which certainly would involve a period of time.

One could also mention that the birds are pretty well left high and dry if this was an evolutionary process, because although the ground is to bear vegetation and the waters the swarms of living creatures, the birds are simply "to fly" with no reference to any source for them. This would fit response to a creative word but not an evolutionary process.

Chapter 2 of Genesis has several points in it which are incompatible with human evolution. First of all there is the creation of Adam. We are told that "the Lord God formed man of dust from the ground, and breathed into his nostrils the breath of life; and man became a living being." If evolution were true, and if Genesis in any way reflects anything that actually did take place, then one would not expect man to be derived from dust but rather from living material. It is worth mentioning that the word translated as dust in the Revised Standard Version is *apar* in the Hebrew. In the Anchor Bible it is described as standing for "lumps of earth, soil, dirt" as well as the resulting particles of dust. The new version translates: "God Yahweh formed man from clods of soil," which to the Jew certainly represented nonliving material. Any hint of origin from living organisms is ruled out by the phrase "man became a living being." In a paper prepared for the Proviso Pastors and Teachers Conference in February of 1962, Paul Bretscher of Concordia Seminary, St. Louis, has the following paragraph: "Man is a distinctive creation; Genesis 1:21 states that God created every living creature (nephesh hayah) which the waters brought forth, and verse 24 states 'That God said let the earth bring forth the living creature (nephesh hayah) . . . of the earth.' Then Genesis 2:7 states, 'And the Lord God formed man . . . and man became a living soul' (nephesh hayah) presumably for the first time. So it would certainly seem from this that man

113

was not derived from any pre-existing line of 'nephesh' or living creatures."

It is significant also that Gen. 2:20 records that man surveyed cattle and birds and beasts of the field but that "for the man there was not found a helper fit for him." Regardless of the literary form of the Genesis account, the message here is loud and clear. Man, Adam, is distinct from all the animals he surveyed, and there was no one like him. This is a completely impossible concept under the theory of evolution, where Adam would have been one of several anthropoid hominids who were approaching the status of homo, through a series of mutations. There would have been many other pre-men and -women like him or at least a number of them. Certainly he would not have surveyed all of the animal kingdom and found no one who would be a helpmeet for him.

This is emphasized by the creation of Eve, which follows, where she is taken from man and recognized as being "at last bone of my bones and flesh of my flesh" (Gen. 2:23). The whole emphasis on sex at this point would again be pure nonsense if theistic evolution were involved, because sex would have originated many, many millions of years previous to this.

It is interesting how some Catholic biologists, who attempt to keep the reality of Adam and Eve and want to accommodate themselves to evolution, wrestle with the problem of the origin of Eve. Fothergill, in his book *Evolution and Christians,* proposes a number of explanations. One is that Adam was "the product of pre-hominid parents acting as instrumental causes." He goes on to say that Adam would have married one of the near-human creatures he lived with. He would then have produced a child which would have been "the product of a fully-formed human male gamete and a near-human female egg. As a single gamete itself contains *all* the potentialities of the offspring, the child would have been human in the true and full sense of the term, and could have received a human soul in the way we all do. It would have been formed *from* the body of Adam in the most natural and intimate way. Such a child could have been Eve.'' He goes on to indicate that Adam then married Eve and thus Eve could be truly spoken of as having been out of Adam.[33] I leave it to you to decide how satisfactory such an explanation might be.

Unless Genesis 1, 2, and 3 are taken as historical and practical, there is no satisfactory explanation of the origin of sin and of death. The continual emphasis on the goodness of creation and man's being created in the image of God does not fit an evolutionary scene. For sin and death and destruction, the law of tooth and fang, the survival of the fittest, would have been a commonplace part of the world from the very beginning. So would have been death. Genesis tells us, as does the New Testament, that sin and death originated through the fall of Adam and Eve. In this connection Alexander Heidel's opinion is worth quoting:

> The presence of the tree of life in the garden of Eden shows that man was intended from the beginning to live forever. Through sin he forfeited this privilege and at the very moment of his transgression entered upon the road of death. Man's state before the fall was not one of absolute immortality, or of absolute freedom from death, in which sense God and the angels are immortal, but rather one of relative or conditional immortality. This could have been turned into absolute immortality by man's eating of the tree of life, which had the power, naturally bestowed upon it by its Creator (2:9), to impart imperishable physical life (3:22). But from this he was prevented after the fall by being banished from the garden, since the acquisition of imperishability by sinful man

would have entailed his continuance in sin forever and would have precluded the possibility of his renewal or restoration. Contrary to F. Schwally, Gen. 3:19 does not attribute the cause of death to the original composition of the human body, so that man would ultimately have died anyway, but states merely one of the consequences of death: Since the human body was formed from the dust of the earth, it shall, upon death, be resolved to earth again. Nowhere in the Old Testament is death regarded as a part of man's God-given constitution, or as the natural end of life. Nor is it indicated anywhere that death already existed before sin but became a punishment through sin.[34]

It is highly interesting that theistic evolutionists are unable to give a satisfactory explanation for this origin of death. Helmut Thielicke, for example, says:

> The dramatic point in our story . . . is that this arrogant man who wanted no limitations put upon him, this man who wanted to snatch God's eternity for himself, who wanted to be immortal and like God, *has his limitations cast into his teeth.* "The man has become like one of us," the story says, "knowing good and evil." After he has nibbled at the tree of knowledge, he will also reach out for the tree of life and plunder the fruit of immortality. He will want to be unlimited in time, he will want to be eternal. And therefore he is driven out of paradise and the burden of mortality is placed upon his back. In other words, the unlimited one is shown his limits.[35]

In other words, Thielicke claims that man was originally mortal and that his sin merely was that he aspired to be immortal in an arrogant attitude. As a consequence, his pre-existent mortality is flung in his face.

Gerhard von Rad, in his commentary, deals with this question of death as a problem when he speaks of various difficulties. In an attempt to explain it from the viewpoint of man already being mortal since his origin was in dust, he stumbles over the fact that then God's threat "you will die" is really meaningless since God did not follow out the threat at that time and extended His grace and permitted him to die later. Since he was to die later anyway, then God obviously did not keep His word. He also regards as exe-getically embarrassing the reference to the tree of life. Why was this in the garden if man was mortal originally and sup-posed to return to the dust and actually has been returning to the dust all along in terms of his ancestors? He speaks of this as a fresh difficulty and says: "Could man after all, after a sentencing, break through the ban of death?" [36]

As Christians and Lutherans we embrace the herme-neutical principle that Scripture is the best interpreter of Scripture and that the New Testament casts light upon the Old. When we apply this to some of these troublesome ques-tions in Genesis, we do not receive any help in connection with the days, which are mentioned only once in the New Testament (Heb. 4:4). However, we do receive considerable emphasis on Adam and Eve—their origin and their experi-ence in the garden, together with the connection this has with the redemptive work of Jesus Christ. Paul speaks of God having "made from one every nation of men to live on all the face of the earth" (Acts 17:26). In 2 Cor. 4:6 Paul talks about the power of the Gospel and says: "It is the God who said, 'Let light shine out of darkness,' who has shone in our hearts to give the light of the knowledge of the glory of God in the face of Christ." In Matt. 19:4-5 Jesus discusses divorce with the Pharisees and replies: "Have you not read that He who made them from the beginning made them male and female and said, 'For this reason a man shall leave his father and mother and be joined to his wife, and the two shall become one'? So they are no longer two but one." In verse 8, in reply to the claim of the Pharisees that Moses allowed divorce, He says: "From the beginning it was not so." This, of course, is a direct reference to the institution of marriage as found in Genesis 2.

More specifically regarding Adam and Eve, Paul takes literally the story of the origin of Eve. This is manifest from the reference in 1 Cor. 11:8-9, where he says: "For man was not made from woman, but woman from man. Neither was man created for woman, but woman for man." And in verse 12, where he says: "For as woman was made from man, so man is now born of woman." In 1 Tim. 2:13-14 Paul writes: "For Adam was formed first, then Eve; and Adam was not deceived, but the woman was deceived and became a transgressor." The word for "formed" is *esplasthe* from *plasso*, which means to form or mold. The word translated "first" is *protos* which Lenski points out is a predicate adjective. He comments: "Adam was created as 'the first.' He existed for some time before Eve was formed." [37] The same position is taken by the Arndt-Gingrich lexicon. It states: "Protos" is used "as a predicate adj., where an adv. can be used in English." It is translated "as the first one." 1 Tim. 2:13 is cited as one example of this usage.[38]

More central is the reference to Adam and his sin as we find it in Romans 5, where Adam is contrasted with Christ. In verse 12 it reads: "Therefore as sin came into the world through one man and death through sin, and so death spread to all men because all men sinned." In verses 17 and 18 it reads: "If, because of one man's trespass, death reigned through that one man, much more will those who receive the abundance of grace and the free gift of righteousness reign in life through the one man Jesus Christ. Then as one man's trespass led to condemnation for all men, so one man's act of righteousness leads to acquittal and life for all men." Walter R. Roehrs points out that this passage as well as the reference in 1 Corinthians leaves no doubt as to the actuality of the fall of Adam and Eve as two individuals who fell from a perfect state and plunged mankind into sin. He says: "Scripture clearly derives the need of all men for a restoration to the primeval relationship to God from the fall of the first parents of man. The actuality of the fall of Adam and Eve, two individuals, is the unargued presupposition for the lost condition of all men and of the necessity of a Savior from sin. The insistence that there is only one Savior is predicated on the fact that there was only one through whom the need of redemption arose. This is the point that is made in 1 Cor. 15: 44-49, 57, as well as in Rom. 5:12, 15-19 (cf. also 1 Tim. 2: 13-14; 1 Cor. 11:8-9)." [39]

The position of Dr. Roehrs is in full agreement with the position of The Lutheran Church—Missouri Synod as reaffirmed at the 46th regular convention in Detroit in June 1965. Resolution 229 says in part: "*Resolved,* That The Lutheran Church—Missouri Synod reaffirms its belief that Adam and Eve were historical persons who fell into sin and were redeemed by our Lord Jesus Christ, and that it abide by its official pronouncement regarding these matters as expressed in the Formula of Concord, Epitome, Art. I; Formula of Concord, Thorough Declaration, Art. I; *Brief Statement,* paragraphs 5, 6, 7." (Detroit *Proceedings,* p. 101)

Anyone who is acquainted with the theory of evolution knows that it is impossible to reconcile with any theory of evolution a historic Adam and Eve who are sinless creatures created in the image of God, not subject to death, and the parents of all mankind. The theory of evolution has no place for the image of God. Man is a brute and arises gradually from a brute ancestry. Death is present at the very beginning. There would have been an evolutionary population, not a single couple such as Adam and Eve. We would conclude then that the concept of theistic evolution is incompatible with the New Testament passages on creation and the fall of man.

One might then go on to ask whether the theory of theistic evolution is philosophically compatible with Christianity.

Before going into this, it is worthwhile to note that the hope for reconciliation between the theory of evolution and Christianity as a supernatural religion is not realized by the compromise of saying that evolution is God's way of creating. If you say that, you then inject into the scientific theory of evolution a supernatural factor.

This is precisely the point made by George Gaylord Simpson. He examines the so-called attempt to inject vitalism or mysticism (his words for God's supernatural guidance of the process) on the part of three famous men: LeComte du Noüy, Edmund W. Sinnott, and Teilhard de Chardin. He concludes: "Three great men and great souls, and all have flatly failed in their quest. It is unlikely that others can succeed where they did not, and surely I know of none who has. The attempt to build an evolutionary theory mingling mysticism and science has only tended to vitiate the science. I strongly suspect that it has been equally damaging on the religious side, but here I am less qualified to judge." [40] Curtly F. Mather of Harvard University makes the same point:

> When a theologian accepts evolution as the process used by the Creator, he must be willing to go all the way with it. Not only is it an orderly process; it is a continuing one. Nothing was "finished" on any "seventh day"; the process of creation is still going

on. The golden age for man — if any — is in the future, not in the past. . . . Moreover, the creative process of evolution is not to be interrupted by any supernatural intervention. . . . The spiritual aspects of the life of man are just as surely a product of the processes called evolution as are his brain and nervous system.[41]

Thus it would appear that if we sacrifice our interpretation of Genesis to naturalism, we are then called upon to go all the way. As a matter of fact a number of evolutionists have been quite clear in the implications which they draw from the process. Julian Huxley has stated: "God is unnecessary." [42] G. G. Simpson has referred to Christianity as a higher form of superstition which in some ways is actually inferior to the superstitions of primitive tribes. He has referred to church services as "higher superstitions celebrated weekly in every hamlet of the United States." [43] In other words, once the premise of evolution is granted that matter interacts with itself under the guidance of the process of natural selection, there is no need of God. Theistic evolutionists of course deny this. In effect they would attempt to baptize the theory and to make it Christian. After two decades of reading evolutionary literature, both philosophical and scientific, I am of the opinion that this baptizing cannot be effected. The theory is based on the interaction of matter with matter. It is based on the changes which are produced by chance and which are then developed by natural selection. If one places God's guidance into the process, he violates one of the basic tenets of the theory. Moreover, evolution has no place for a man starting in a good world, a man starting with a knowledge of righteousness and true holiness (Eph. 4:24; Col. 3:10). Man does not fall from a lofty position. Rather he is climbing upward under his own power from a lower position and achieving a higher one. This is the basic rationale of evolution and cannot be separated from it.

That this is not my personal bias can be demonstrated by several sources. Paul Raubiczak, a professor of philosophy at Cambridge University, in his book *Existentialism — For and Against* (Cambridge University Press, 1964), points out that the Darwinian theory and its descendants have many gaps. The theory does not explain the origin of matter. It does not explain the irregularity in matter which is necessary for certain of the cosmological theories from the viewpoint of its origin. It does not explain the origin of purpose. It does not explain the origin of life and the different quality of the human mind. He then states: "The theory of evolution shows, as do all theories, the limitations of knowledge. It should not therefore be accepted as a complete basis for philosophy, or as ultimate absolute truth. Scientists are fully entitled to make it the basis of research, but philosophers should consider its limitations critically." (P. 23)

Raubiczak continues:

> Nevertheless evolution has been made the basis of a complete philosophy. It provided philosophers with a metaphysical and ethical system, thus deeply influencing their ideas about the nature of man and his behavior. In fact, the philosophy based on Darwinism has exercised an extremely strong influence, far beyond the realms of science and philosophy, upon the whole development of European thought. The ruthless life and death struggle for survival has been translated into a new morality, as ruthless competition in a capitalist society, as ruthless warfare in the communist world, and as ruthless nationalism everywhere. Moreover, for the first time in human history, mind and reason are no longer seen as some mysterious higher power, as part of a supernatural,

divine sphere breaking in upon human existence, but as the product of lower, biological factors, and nothing has done more to fortify materialism. The word spirit has lost all its meaning, and human mind itself has been impoverished. (P. 23)

Raubiczak goes on to discuss Nietzsche. He asserts that Nietzsche in his philosophy is dependent upon Darwinism and its philosophy: "Nietzsche's next step fits in once more with the demands of philosophical Darwinism: God has to be dismissed as well. He emphasizes again and again, 'God is dead,' and asks rhetorically, 'What thinker still needs the hypothesis of God?'" (p. 28). Raubiczak also asserts that Nietzsche's theory of heredity shows the influence of Darwinism and his philosophy. He continually demands the breeding of a new master race and the prohibition for its sake of the reproduction of all the discontented, the rancorous, and the grudging, the sterilization of criminals and the annihilation of millions of misfits. Raubiczak says: "The spectre of the Nazi gas chambers looms behind such statements . . . we must not forget that it is not only Nietzsche's philosophy, but also the theory of evolution which leads to such consequences." (Pp. 35 – 36)

It is hardly necessary to point out the unchristian and unbiblical nature of the entire tenor of the philosophy of evolution. It is evident from the writings of evolutionists, both in the area of science and in the area of philosophy, that this philosophy can no more be separated from the theory than dye can be separated when a sweater has been permanently dyed a given color. It becomes a part of the very warp and woof of the substance. When an attempt at separation is made, the cry of vitalism and supernaturalism is made by the scientists on the one hand; on the other hand, it is evident theologically that basic doctrines such as the nature of man, the origin of death, original sin, etc., are placed in jeopardy if not denied completely.

The final question concerning theistic evolution is this: Is it Lutheran? If by Lutheran we mean does it agree with any of the exegesis of Martin Luther on the Book of Genesis, then the answer is of course an emphatic "No!" We sometimes forget that in Luther's day there was a great attempt to allegorize or figuratively interpret large sections of the Bible. Some of the fathers were not above attempting this with the Genesis account. Concerning this, Luther remarks: "This also has a bearing on our firmly holding the conviction that there were really six days on which the Lord created everything, in contrast to the opinion of Augustine and Hilary, who believed that everything was created in a single moment. They, therefore, abandon the historical account, pursuing allegories and fabricating I don't know what speculations" (*LW*, 1, 121). In another section Luther says: "It was very difficult for me to break away from my habitual zeal for allegory; and yet I was aware that allegories were empty speculations and the froth, as it were, of the Holy Scriptures. It is the historical sense alone which supplies the true and sound doctrine" (*LW*, 1, 233). A little later (*LW*, 1, 237) he adds: "Nobody can fail to see that Moses does not intend to present allegories but simply to write the history of the primitive world."

Creation as a Corollary to Justification by Faith

In answering the question: Is theistic evolution Lutheran? we can learn from an unpublished essay by Walter R. Roehrs in which he describes creation as a "corollary of justification by faith." Under this heading he lists six points.

    1. The Christian religion is a historical religion also in this respect that justification by faith accepts on faith the revelation that through a historical event

the need for a reconciliation with God arose, which God met in the life, death, and resurrection of His incarnate Son.

2. It is only through a divinely created faith that the reconciled and justified Christians understand "that the world was created by the word of God, so that what is seen was made out of things which do not appear" and that God is "blessed Father of us all."

3. Faith accepts the divine revelation that there would have been no need for justification by grace through faith if man had remained as God created him: in the image of God and in a blessed communion with Him.

4. Both the Old Testament and the New Testament teach that "by one man sin entered into the world and death by sin" thus breaking man's communion with God.

5. Because all men are "in the image of" this one man cursed by sin, they can be justified from absolute separation from God only when they are justified by grace through faith.

6. God, who made one man in His image, will restore all reconciled and believing men to the image that he had lost.

The Lutheran Confessions Concerning Our First Parents

Robert D. Preus, of Concordia Seminary, St. Louis, states:

There is not the slightest doubt that the confessions receive as actual history and fact the story of Adam and Eve in Genesis 2 (FC, Ep I, 4; SD, I, 9, 27). Adam and Eve were the first two people of this world — placed by God in the Garden of Eden. Adam and Eve

125

were created with body and soul (FC, Ep I, 4), according to Gen. 2:7; they were created in the image of God (according to Gen. 1:27), which consisted in a wisdom and righteousness being "implanted in man that would grasp God and reflect Him, that is, that man received gifts like the knowledge of God, fear of God, and trust in God" (Ap II, 17—18). Here Gen. 2:7 is definitely interpreted according to Col. 3: 10 and Eph. 4:24 (*analogia fidei*—analogy of faith). There is no attempt to interpret Gen. 1:27 independently of the New Testament. These two people, Adam and Eve, were originally created pure, good, and holy, as the Genesis account says (FC, SD, I, 27). Furthermore, marriage was established between Adam and Eve, and this cannot be nullified as a God-pleasing institution (AC, XXIII, 8; cf. Matt. 19:4 ff.).[44]

Preus continues:

We notice here at once that the historical fact of the Fall is never questioned (FC, SD, I, 23, 9); "the dough out of which God forms and makes man has been corrupted and perverted in Adam" (FC, SD, I, 38). We notice also that Satan is the instigator of sin, the one who "corrupted God's handiwork in Adam" (FC, SD, I, 42, 7, 27). . . . Third, we notice the connection, alluded to so often (FC, SD, I, 28, 9, 11, 13; Ap II, 5, 2; AC, II, 1), between Adam's sin (fall) and our sinful condition, that since the fall of Adam all men who are propagated according to nature are born in sin (AC II, 1) and that our sin is a hereditary condition *(Erbsünde)* which we have by conception and birth (Ap II, 6, 11, 8, 23). This connection, which is not drawn from Genesis 3 but from Romans 5; Matt. 15:19; Gen. 8:21; 6:5 and other passages, although never explained, is nevertheless real and is an article of faith. Again we notice how the New Testament is simply brought in to interpret the Old Testament. Barth's doctrine of *Ursünde,* that every man is his own Adam, would be totally untenable. In other words, the actuality of the Fall is the basis of the actuality of original sin today. (Pp. 19–20)

The Lutheran Confessions also teach that bodily death was introduced by the sin of Adam. (Our italics in the following.)

   a. The Apology (II 46-47): "Genesis describes another penalty for original sin. There human nature is subjected not only *to death and other physical ills,* but also to the rule of the devil. For there this fearful sentence is pronounced, "I will put enmity between you and the woman, and between your seed and her seed" (Gen. 3:15). The deficiency and concupiscence are sin as well as penalty; *death, other physical ills,* and the tyranny of the devil are, in the precise sense, penalties." (Tappert, p. 106)

   b. The Smalcald Articles (III, I 1): "Here we must confess what St. Paul says in Rom. 5:12, namely, that sin had its origin in one man, Adam, through whose disobedience all men were made sinners and became *subject to death* and the devil." (Tappert, p. 302)

   c. The Formula of Concord (SD I 13): "The punishment and penalty of original sin which God imposes upon Adam's children and upon original sin is death, eternal damnation, together with *other bodily,* spiritual, temporal, and eternal *misery,* the tyranny and dominion of the devil. . . ." (Tappert, p. 511)

Quite clearly the Confessions teach that "death of body" came through Adam's fall!

Preus states: "We note also that the *theological significance* of Genesis 1 – 3 is for the Lutheran Symbols dependent wholly on the factuality of the account. This means that there is in Genesis 1 – 3 a description of something actually happening. A nondescriptive account of Genesis 1 – 3 (e. g., a demythologized poem sung to God's glory; an aetiological saga; a mere cosmology purified of theogony, theomachy, and other unworthy elements; a reworking of various older Hebrew or other myths) would be totally uncongenial to the Lutheran Confessions as being opposed to the serious theological purpose of the section and to the analogy of faith." [45]

It is evident from Preus's analysis of the Confessions that it is not Lutheran to accept theistic evolution. The Confessions build their doctrine of man's fall and of the redemption by Christ on the Genesis account as providing the springboard for the necessity of redemption. To substitute the philosophy of evolution, that man has developed from lower forms of life, that he gradually developed the concept of God and the concept of right and wrong, that he is becoming better and better, is to fly in the face of Scripture and of the Lutheran Confessions. To attempt to say that there was a real Adam and Eve, but that their bodies were created by an evolutionary process, is to attempt an unhappy mating of evolution and creation which is logically inconsistent and doomed to failure. Nor will it win the desired approval of the evolutionary scientist.

It would seem better to accept in simple faith the account of the origin of man as given in the Book of Genesis, to allow scientists to continue to pursue their research, but to insist on what Scripture tells us concerning man's origin and his purpose in life as well as the redemption which God has wrought for us in Jesus Christ. It would be tragic if we were to permit scientific theories, scientific philosophies, to dictate our theology either explicitly or implicitly. Let us really let the Scriptures speak to us and not attempt to read into them many things which even liberal commentaries insist the authors never thought of.

Genesis 3: The Fall of Man

The Genesis account moves swiftly from cosmic creation, the creation of man, the perfect state, to the catastrophe of the fall of Adam and Eve. Genesis 3 is freighted with theological significance, for it shows the event which turned man into a condemned, perverted enemy of God. It sets forth the theological basis for the necessity of the redemptive act of Christ.

Here too there are sharply debated theological issues. For the folklore of ancient peoples contains many elements that bear a strange resemblance to the story of Genesis 3. Greek mythology has the legend of a monstrous sea serpent that attacks a maiden who is rescued by Perseus. The Polynesian area in the Pacific has no snakes. But elements of the story are played by a monster eel which is reminiscent of the snake in Eden. The Mayan-Aztec and Peruvian cultures have a mythological figure of a cosmic tree with an eagle at its summit and a serpent at its root with godlike figures guarding it. Joseph Cambell, in his book on primitive mythology, points out that the story of the serpent and the maiden is practically as early as "the first appearance of Homo sapiens on the prehistoric scene." [46]

As one moves closer to Israel, the parallels to Genesis 3 are more striking. The Egyptians had the legend of Apophis, the archenemy of God. Apophis was the devil par excellence, represented sometimes as a serpent and sometimes as a crocodile. The Babylonians had the myth of Adapa, said by some to be a parallel to Adam. Adapa like Adam loses the gift of immortality, although it is by refusing to eat food offered to him and by obeying a command rather than violating one. The Babylonians also have the story of Gilgamesh, who was cheated out of immortality by the serpent when he lost the rejuvenating plant.

These striking elements of similarity have moved some people to claim that the Genesis account is merely an exalted version of the myths of their neighbors in the ancient Near East. It is regarded, then, as an elevated myth, teaching a religious truth, but with no correspondence to fact.

Such a judgment must be rejected as unfounded. E. O. James, in his book on Myth and Ritual in the Ancient Near East, points out that there is, first of all, "no comparable Babylonian or Sumerian version of either Eden or the Fall of man. The setting of the Garden was Palestinian rather than Mesopotamian, and the events leading up to the expulsion are only very remotely connected with the myth of Adapa and the Gilgamesh epic, confined for the most part to the loss of immortality through the guile of the serpent." [47]

The late Alexander Heidel in his book The Babylonian Genesis has analyzed the two accounts, that is, the Babylonian and the Hebrew. His conclusion is that there are similarities, particularly in figures of speech and terms perhaps derived from foreign literature, but that there is no essential dependence of Genesis on the Babylonian myths. He points out in each case vital differences which place the accounts "as far apart as the antipodes." Heidel asserts:

> So far no evidence for the first sin has been found any-where in Babylonian or Assyrian literature. If it is at all permissible to speak of a fall, it was a fall of the gods, not of man. . . . In Genesis man is created in the image of God; but the Babylonians, like the Greeks and Romans, created their gods in the image of man. . . .

130

> Since all the gods were evil by nature and since man
> was formed with their blood, man of course inherited
> their evil nature. Man, consequently, was *created*
> evil and was evil from his very beginning. How, then,
> could he fall? The idea that man fell from a state of
> moral perfection does not fit into the system of
> Babylonian speculation.[48]

Heidel also states that such similarities as do exist between the Biblical and the Babylonian accounts of creation and the experiences of man in losing immortality may possibly be explained on the basis that both versions have sprung from a common source of some kind. The late Ira M. Price, of the University of Chicago, attributed the common elements to a common inheritance of man going back to "a time when the human race occupied a common home and held a common faith." (Heidel, p. 117)

If a slight digression may be permitted, it is interesting that the literature of mythology distinguishes myths, at least of a certain type, from fiction. Malinowski, an expert in the field, claims: "Myth is not of the nature of fiction . . . but it is a living reality, believed to have once happened in primeval times, and continuing ever since to influence the world and human destinies."[49] This is not to say that the many myths of ancient peoples are all factual and free from error or fiction. On the contrary, they are loaded with embellishments. But they do relate what was thought to have really and truly taken place in the distant past. Is it strange, then, that echoes of creation, the fall of man, and the flood are to be found around the globe?

But is the Genesis account mythical? We have pointed out that it is radically distinct from other accounts of the first man and the coming of death into the world. Let us now briefly add the thought that it is free of mythical content.

Some claim that words out of Genesis 1 like *tehom* for the "deep" are related to "Tiamat," the name for an ancient Babylonian goddess involved in the Gilgamesh epic. But there is no more significance to this than our use of "Wednesday" and "Thursday." We surely no longer think of them as days devoted to the gods Woden and Thor. Dr. Childs of Yale's Divinity School has written: "The word 'tehom' has retained its feminine and undetermined form but now only as a vestige without significance. The independent life once in the word has been 'demythologized' to such an extent that without the parallels from comparative religion, its mythical origin would have passed unnoticed." [50]

Concerning the snake in Genesis 3 Childs writes: "The serpent was not co-existent from the beginning with God. He was merely a creature who owed his existence, as did all other life, to God. The myth of a primeval principle of evil within the world was flatly rejected." (P. 49)

Much more could be said. However, by now it should be evident that we can come to the text of Genesis 3 and treat it as an inspired account of man's actual fall from the perfect state—an account with tremendous meaning for our state of sin by nature today.

Theological Significance

The theological significance of all this dare not be underevaluated. Many have attempted to state it. Weiser in a famous statement says: "The problem that the Yahwist investigates is the enigmatic fact that man does not adopt an unambiguous attitude toward his life, but faces it in extremely remarkable ambiguity. . . . The thought of death cripples the will to live; work, although recognized as the purport of life, becomes misery because of toil and failure; the happiness of motherhood, the highest fulfillment of a woman's life, is troubled by pain and sorrow. Only with broken bearing does man face his life; that is the enigmatic fact which the Yahwist contemplates and intends to explain by the narrative of Gen. chs. 2 f." [51]

All this is true, but it is inadequate if one stops there. The Formula of Concord (SD I 13) goes to the heart of the matter in a passage we have quoted before: "The punishment and penalty of original sin which God imposes upon Adam's children and upon original sin is death, eternal damnation, together with other bodily, spiritual, temporal, and eternal misery, the tyranny and dominion of the devil. . . . (Tappert, p. 511)

But if Genesis 3 contains the curse of God upon the serpent, man, woman, and the earth, there is also the promise. To the serpent God says: "I will put enmity between you and the woman, and between your seed and her Seed. He shall bruise your head, and you shall bruise His heel." (Gen. 3:15)

This has long been known as the "protevangelium," the first Gospel promise. Concerning this passage the Lutheran Confessions state (Ap XII 53): "This promise [the Gospel] is repeated continually throughout Scripture; first it was given to Adam [in Gen. 3:15], later to the patriarchs, then illumined by the prophets." (Tappert, p. 189)

Some theologians, however, have taken exception to this identification of Gen. 3:15 with a promise of deliverance of the human race through Christ. They hold that it is merely a statement of general grace, that it merely indicates that God is not going to execute His threat of death, that it is merely an "enmity oracle" pointing to a struggle to come, but nothing more.

Over against this position and in favor of the position long held in the church that Gen. 3:15 and the "seed of the woman" do indeed point to Christ, we may note that the Hebrew text substantiates the traditional interpretation. In the Old Testament a head wound such as that promised the serpent was regarded as fatal, while a heel wound would not be. This in itself indicates victory for the Seed of the woman. Moreover, Adam gives Eve a name of hope. She is called "the mother of all living." Furthermore, the "seed" is designated as that of the woman, not that of the man. This again is unusual and is fully consonant with the subsequently revealed virgin birth.

To add to the evidence, the Hebrew word for seed *(dzera)* is often used of individuals and need not refer to a group. The ancient Greek translation of the Old Testament, the Septuagint, so understood it. Although this version translates the Hebrew word *dzera* as *to sperma* (neuter), it then translates the Hebrew pronoun *hu,* not as neuter but as masculine *(autos).* This is also done in the modern English translation, the Revised Standard Version. We may also note that the Hebrew verb *jeshuphenu* for "shall crush" has a masculine suffix. All of this adds up to a good case for understanding "seed" as pointing to one individual rather than to "seed" in general as indicating all of Eve's progeny. Indeed, "seed" is used in this individualized sense in a number of passages, for instance: Gen. 4:25; 1 Sam. 1:11; 2 Sam. 7:12.

To these thoughts may be added the fact that the Bible knows of grace only through the work of Jesus Christ. There is no other way. Certainly the Israelites for whom Genesis was first written already knew of the covenant grace of God through the promises to Abraham and the fathers. Certainly the promise to Eve would have been meaningful to them in this context.

Albertus Pieters in his *Notes on Genesis* (Grand Rapids: Eerdmans, 1943) has put it well. He writes: "It [i. e., Gen. 3:15] is not Messianic in form, which is perhaps the reason why it is not quoted as such in the New Testament; but it is Messianic in essence: We see at once that it is so when we remember that the 'seed of the woman' must have a leader in this conflict, that such a leader has been found in the Lord Jesus Christ, and that He was born of a virgin; thus fitting as no one else ever can fit the unique description: the 'seed of the woman.' '' (P. 88)

Concluding Statement

In conclusion may it be said that many problems exist in theology. The great lessons of the Bible are clear and beyond disputing: the almighty power and overarching goodness of the Creator who is also the Preserver, the depravity and desperate need of man, the incomprehensible love of God and our redemption in Jesus Christ, the great commission to go out and make disciples of all nations. These great truths with all the vast complex of supporting Christian theology come to us alone by revelation in Holy Scripture.

Problems of interpretation and application we have. Study them we can and must. But let us avoid the folly of adding to God's Word or of subtracting from it. Man's mind dare not sit in judgment on God's revelation, not even today. If it does, in our presumption we may nibble away at the outer fringes until we find ourselves attacking the very central truths. May we indeed use Scripture as Christ and the apostles used the Old Testament—without reservation and with the utter confidence implicit in the sacred formula, "It is written."

As Jesus once said: "You search the Scriptures because you think that in them you have eternal life, and it is they that bear witness of Me" (John 5:39). But let us not stop there. Rather in continuous repentance and in faith let us come to Him as the Savior whom we accept also into our hearts; lest we come under the condemnation of the next verse: "Yet you refuse to come to Me that you may have life." (John 5:40)

Soli deo gloria

There Was Evening
—and There Was Morning

Richard G. Korthals, M. S.

"In the beginning God created the heavens and the earth. The earth was without form and void, and darkness was upon the face of the deep; and the Spirit of God was moving over the face of the waters. And God said, 'Let there be light'; and there was light. And God saw that the light was good; and God separated the light from the darkness. God called the light Day, and the darkness He called Night. And there was evening and there was morning, one day." (Gen. 1:1-5)

> Away out there alone, above,
> Without a thing to make it of,
> The world was made without a flaw,
> Without a hammer or a saw,
> Without a bit of wood or stone,
> Without a bit of flesh or bone,
> Without a board or nail or screw,
> Or anything to nail it to.
> Without a foothold or a trace
> Of anything at all but space.
> The only thing the Lord could do

Was simply speak a word or two.

And if the story told is true,

The world came boldly into view. (Author Unknown)

And if the story told is true . . . Two centuries ago the mere hint that this story could possibly be false would have been sufficient to brand the speaker a heretic. Today the acceptance of this story of the creation as true can result in the word "fool" being attached to your name. Why has this almost violent change in attitude taken place—and who, if anybody, is correct?

The why can probably best be answered by quoting a recent Life Nature Library publication entitled *Evolution*. The following is written on page 10 concerning evolution:

Darwin did not invent the concept. But when he started his career, the doctrine of special creation could be doubted only by heretics. When he finished, the fact of evolution could be denied only by the abandonment of reason. He demolished the old theory with two books. One published in 1859, he titled "On the Origin of Species by Means of Natural Selection, or the Preservation of Favored Races in the Struggle for Life." The second, published in 1871, he called "The Descent of Man, and Selection in Relation to Sex."

The books did not so much undermine the old, comfortable order of things as simply overwhelm it; nobody had ever bothered to try documenting the other side—instantaneous creation—with such a painstakingly built structure of evidence. At two strokes Darwin gave modern science a rationale, a philosophy, an evolutionary, and thereby revolutionary, way of thinking about the universe and everything in it, and incidentally established himself as the Newton of biology. But at the same time he dealt mankind's preening self-esteem a body blow from which it may never recover, and for which Darwin may never be quite forgiven. For it is one thing for man to be told (and want to believe) that he was created in the literal image of God. It is quite another for him to be told (and have to accept) that he is, while unique, merely the culmination of a billion years of ever-evolving life, and that he must trace his godhood down a gnarled and twisted family tree through mammals and amphibians to the lowly fish and thence to some anonymous, if miraculous, Adam molecule.

Was Darwin right? Is the world, and its inhabitants, the result of a cosmic accident? Are we the descendants of some lower order of mammal, and as such then constantly evolving into a more perfect form of mankind? If we realize that Darwin was a scientist, committed to the method of science, *and if we accept this method,* then we must answer yes to the question regarding evolution. It is very evident in studying history that Darwin was a product of his time, a time when science came into its own. Had Darwin not developed the concept of evolution, somebody else would have. Therefore, if I must think as a pure scientist, committed only to using the methods of science, then I must agree with him — I really have little choice.

Should our church then reexamine its position on creation? Are we justified in having people research Biblical documents line by line, word by word, letter by letter, looking for hidden and obscure meanings which would enable us to reinterpret the first chapters of Genesis? Is a well-known Bible study course correct when it spends an entire lesson on the discussion of the various forms of Biblical writing, namely historical, poetical, personification, fable, allegory, imagery, and symbolism, a discussion which is carried out in order that this question can then be asked concerning Genesis 2 and 3: "What literary medium do we find here, historical event in poetic form, imagery-personification? Whatever our findings, barring a wooden literalism, our conclusions on the overarching message of this portion of Scripture will be the same."

Must we continue in our attempt to modify Scriptural interpretation so as to bring about agreement with scientific theories, changing days to eons, miracles to modified natural events? Perhaps theologians may disagree, but my answer to all of these questions, my answer as a layman with a strong belief in my religion, is a resounding no. I feel a conservative position — literal interpretation — on creation and miracles is as justified today as it was centuries ago. I can see no reason for a change.

I imagine that if I could examine each of your minds right now I would find this thought present: "Well, here is a real two-faced individual — a true middle-of-the-roader, fence-riding type. First he says it is, and then it isn't — first that evolution is true, and then that the literal interpretation of Genesis is true. Come now, it must be one or the other."

I agree with you, it must be one or the other. If you are puzzled, then it is because you missed the fact that I prefaced my statements of agreement with the method of analysis being used. In the one case it was scientific, in the other religious. This question of methodology, and the implications it carries, is in my estimation the crux of the entire problem. To explain why, I would like to review something you are undoubtedly already familiar with, but which is so important to our understanding that we should have a common ground from which to start. This is the definition of what many outstanding philosophers feel are the three main kinds, spheres, or domains of knowledge. These are philosophy, science, and religion. Let us begin by defining science and describing its limitations.

If we were looking for one word which would best describe the methods of science, it would be "investigate." All sciences look into things and discover data which are not a part of the common experience of mankind. Now what do I mean by this "common experience of mankind"? By this I mean the experiences that you and I, our ancestors, our children, men of all times and ages have in common — experiences we have simply by being awake, not looking for anything, not observing any method. If I clap my hands, snap my fingers, drop a book, you know subconsciously what has happened, even if you didn't witness the event. We have all seen and heard a storm, seen things grow and die, observed changes in nature, watched things move. These are simple experiences which everyone has had; they are the common experiences of mankind.

If you stay with the common experiences of mankind, you will never develop a science. Science deals with that which is on the periphery — outside the common experiences of mankind. It investigates using telescope, microscope, photographic emulsion, or nuclear reaction. A scientist forms a hypothetical theory as to why something happens, and then sets out to prove it is correct by conducting experiment upon experiment, using special equipment such as mentioned previously. The experiences which he has are generally limited to a small number of people; they are uncommon, or unique, experiences.

If we were then to define the tools, or the methods, of science, we would say they are observations which affect the senses of the observer — senses such as sight, smell, touch, or hearing — causing sensations which he must then analyze and formulate, using his power of reason. Because this is the method of science, it is limited to describing — not *explaining why,* but *describing how.* Science by its method stays on the surface of reality, dealing with the apparent or phenomenal, and as a result there are a host of questions which it cannot answer.

Take a very simple question in which you may be interested, one concerning knowledge. What are the different kinds of knowledge? What does it mean to know? How do you know? What is knowing in itself? We could investigate from now till the end of time and not answer these questions. You can answer them by thinking, but not by looking.

Neither can science answer questions which require placing a value on something. It cannot tell you whether your occupation is good or bad, whether a society is exemplary or corrupt. And science will never develop to the extent where it can answer these questions. These are questions which are beyond the competence of scientific inquiry—the method used is inadequate, inappropriate.

This is not to say that science is bad, for this would be far from the truth. Science is extremely useful, but its utility lies in its ability to produce—the production of goods and services which contribute to the mastery of the physical world. Because of this ability, science is powerful; but it is a tremendous power that by itself cannot and does not tell us where to go or what to do.

Philosophy, on the other hand, produces nothing physical, and yet it also serves a high purpose—a good—in that it can answer many of the questions which science cannot touch. The philosopher makes use of the common experiences of mankind in attempting to describe the reason behind all events. Philosophy and philosophical inquiries are not investigative. The philosopher needs no data, no special instruments. He is an armchair thinker who can sit in a dark room and contemplate the common experiences of mankind. His question is not how things operate, but rather what they are—and why they are as we find them. At first it would appear that he has little value, since nothing physical comes out of this room—he doesn't make anything. However, if we use this line of reasoning, then there are many things which have no value. As an example, consider a road map. It contains knowledge, yet it never makes anything. Yet that map can become our most precious possession when we are in strange territory, for it directs us where to go (if we can read it).

Science is concerned with phenomena. Philosophy delves into the what, the why of things—the underlying existence. In science reason serves sense. In philosophy sense serves reason—the main work is done by reason, not sense. Because of this, the very questions science cannot answer, philosophy can. As an example, suppose you all ask yourselves this question: "What is the difference between science and philosophy?" You can agree with what I have said, or you can say that all this is wrong and instead give some other answer. But if you give any answer to that question at all, then you do it as a philosopher, not as a scientist. There is no method whereby you can scientifically answer that question. Just pause and think for a moment. Could you possibly—by any means of investigation, experiment, or laboratory research—discover the difference between science and philosophy? Obviously not!

Philosophy can solve the questions which require the establishment of values. The philosopher can answer questions concerning human happiness—whether a form of government is good or bad, a war just or unjust, your job beneficial or harmful to mankind. He can demonstrate that democracy is, in terms of justice, the only perfectly just form of government. These are questions that are philosophical, but totally untouchable by the methods of science.

So much for science and philosophy, their methods and equipment, usefulness, and limitations. Now where does the third realm of knowledge—namely, religion—fit into this picture. What is its method, its usefulness? If there is religion, distinct as a body of knowledge, practically and speculatively, then what would it be like? There is no distinction possible between religion on one hand and science and philosophy on the other, unless that distinction is made in the separate realms of faith as opposed to reason. Allow me to explain what I mean. Over here, science and philosophy are both knowledge, obtainable by the exercise of man's faculties, his mind, his senses, and his reason. Whatever man obtains is gotten through his own efforts. He observes, analyzes, invents techniques, and performs experiments — acquiring knowledge through his own hard work — using his natural faculties.

If religion is nothing but some other form of inquiry using natural means, then it can be reduced to these two. For religion to be distinct, it must consist of knowledge which man receives but does not acquire by his own efforts — and is this not the definition of revelation? True religion claims to say something which could not possibly be said if it had not been revealed by God. It does not claim to have arrived at this knowledge by investigation, historical analysis, or historical research. It claims to have received it as a gift of God.

Religion, having this revelation, this gift from God, is enabled through this means to answer questions which the scientist and philosopher cannot begin to touch. It could, as examples to these questions, take the Christian doctrines of the Trinity or the Incarnation — but I don't want to. Instead I would like to take a doctrine which you may feel does not belong in this class, the doctrine of creation. Neither philosopher nor scientist can tell with the slightest degree of certainty whether or not the world had a beginning. As a Christian, however, you have an answer. You know the world began — it had a beginning — for God has chosen to reveal to you the answer. That answer is found in the first verse of the first chapter of Genesis: "In the beginning God created the heaven and the earth." It is an answer which is impossible to prove by reason or investigation. If you have an answer to that question, then you have it on the basis of your religion, your religious faith.

This means that a body of knowledge can be properly classified as a religion only if this faith is present. If you do not admit to faith, then forget religion. Following Christ as a great moral leader and teacher, even imitating His exemplary character, is not religion. You might as well follow the moral teachings of Socrates, for all you have is a moral philosophy.

Three bodies of knowledge, each separate and distinct, each with a method, each with a purpose, each with limitations. On the basis of this common understanding let us now go back and reexamine the questions asked earlier—and the answers given.

What about the statement made to the effect that if we realize that Darwin was a scientist, and if we accept his method, then we must agree with him? Did we not just agree that only religion could answer questions concerning the beginning of the world? Yes, this is true, for Darwin was stepping out of his field of competence in attempting to answer this question—science was overstepping its boundaries. Then doesn't agreement with Darwin and those following him indirectly acknowledge acceptance of the unbiblical theory of evolution? Yes it does—if, and please notice this key phrase— *if we accept the application of his method to this question.* Let me explain why.

For a moment imagine that you are a pure scientist, committed to using only the methods of science. This will mean using only observable data—and your senses and reason to interpret it. You have never heard of the Bible—and even if you did, your method forbids the use of this knowledge. As you are sitting in your seat, you let your thoughts stray and you begin to think and wonder about the origin of the world and its inhabitants. You know you must depend upon data and reason, but this doesn't trouble you, for you are well trained, highly intelligent, and have a wealth of data at your disposal. And so you start correlating facts, forming hypotheses, making assumptions. You look at the world's inhabitants around you, noting differences and similarities—seeing the effects of mutations, the results of hybrids. You see dairy cattle producing twice as much milk as their ancestors, blocky beef cattle as opposed to the rangy Texas Longhorn—all changes which have been brought about because of selective breeding. You see horses of sturdier stock, chickens which lay only large white eggs, children who are larger than their parents. Suddenly the thought comes to you that everything is improving, is evolving from some lower and less perfect form—suddenly you have the key, a hypothetical answer to the question of the origin of life. You see with clarity that everything seen on earth today has evolved from some lower form of life. But where do you start? You, as a scientist, can only use the laws of nature present around you, and using these you extrapolate back through time to the only place where you can stop—a single cell, formed by pure chance. You—restricted to using only the methods of science—have no choice.

You have formed your hypothesis, your theory or idea. Now you must substantiate it. First you realize that the process you are visualizing and proposing is extremely slow; therefore the world must be billions of years old. How can you show this? Well, if you say that the earth was formed as a smooth, homogeneous ball, then you can look at the Grand Canyon and calculate the millions of years it took the Colorado River to carve this chasm from the smooth surface. Your estimate is made using the present measurable erosion rates as your yardstick.

You also realize that you must show that a common tie exists between various forms of animal life. You notice that there is a similarity between some bone structures—for instance the two bones present in the forearms of many animals. Backbones are similar, as are the fetal forms in some instances. You propose that this is evidence demonstrating that the animals—including man—must have a common ancestor. Ancient fossil remains are found in rocks. In some cases you use the rocks to establish the age of fossil remains; in other cases, where there is an apparent discontinuity in the rock structure, the fossil establishes the age of the rocks. You use these fossils as evidence that at one time this was the only form of life which existed—and therefore everything must have evolved from it.

So you—in your own mind, using only your reason to evaluate data—gradually develop your theory. True, there are many gaps in your observations, ideas which you cannot substantiate with actual evidence; but as you go along you make what you feel are reasonable assumptions to complete the picture, to a certain extent using your imagination. With the pattern developing, you decide to consolidate your thoughts by putting them in writing. Then, at your friend's persuasion, you write a book—which is eagerly read by all who have been looking for a solution for this particularly difficult problem of dealing with origins. Soon other books are written—some by psuedo scientists who popularize your complex theory in a paperback version—and who in the process somehow have forgotten to put in the "ifs" which you so carefully included. So suddenly the assumptions you made—the guesses and the musings, the dreams and the imaginations—these suddenly become fact, and anyone who doesn't believe them is either obstinate or biased. You find yourself a celebrity, acclaimed by all for having found the answer to the mystery surrounding the question of man's origin.

"But," you say, "I don't want to go back that far. I will

base part of my theory on Biblical knowledge, and will assume that at least man was created." How can you — for remember our initial agreement? You are a pure scientist, utilizing only the methods which that body of knowledge can use. Therefore you cannot stop at that point in time — you have no justification for such an assumption — no valid reason. You must go back to a single cell, because your reason tells you — after evaluating available evidence — that man could not instantaneously be created out of nothing. There is no scientific data to substantiate this — nor is there an experiment which you can perform which will duplicate it. It is against every law of nature in existence today — and these laws are the tools of your trade, immutable laws which you use to project present-day findings into the past. The very idea is unreasonable and incomprehensible.

This is true not only with respect to the question of the origin of life; you must also assume that the earth started out as a homogeneous sphere, smooth and untarnished, with all elements in their most basic form. You really have no choice, for where else can you start? Could you say that the Grand Canyon was 1,000 feet deep when the world was formed — or 1,627 feet deep — or that it had a depth of 2,369 feet? You must start somewhere — and that somewhere must be a smooth surface if you are to substantiate your arguments.

So now do you see why the methods of science dictate an evolutionary theory? Reason, senses, and observable data all tell us there can be no other way. If you were all scientists I would stop right here, for though you may have different ideas concerning the details, yet the basic concept is one you would accept and uphold.

But you are not scientists, you are people with religious beliefs — people who not only use reason but also have faith in God's revelation to us. As such you are told in the revealed Word that the earth was created by God and that He created

147

us in His image, breathed into our nostrils the breath of life. As a result of this knowledge a struggle exists in your mind, a mental conflict which says you should accept one or the other idea, but not both. Which will it be?

Much hinges on the validity of scientific claims—the amount of truth which can be attached to the theories presently being advanced. Let me state now that the theory of evolution will never—in my estimation—be completely disproved. In fact, evolution does take place—we can see it in nature around us. God did not necessarily create all the varieties of dogs, cats, and even humans which are present in the world today. Most of these evolved. But I firmly believe that He did create one of each "kind"—biologically speaking. The theory that things evolved from a single source and that the rattlesnake, butterfly, eagle, whale, and man all have the same common ancestor is far from proved. This is evidenced by the fact that scientists themselves have trouble finding a theory which is agreeable to all.

I have neither the space nor the ability to present all the arguments against single-source evolution. I am neither a biologist, a geologist, nor a paleontologist. However, as an engineer familiar with scientific methods, I would like to explain to you several general weaknesses.

First let us examine the question of assumptions. How can these lead us astray? Let me give you a very simple example. Suppose we are going down an interstate highway in the middle of the desert, miles from nowhere, at 11 o'clock in the morning, and come upon a car which has just run out of gas and is standing deserted. The question arises as to how many hours the man had been driving since his last gas stop, since it is considered a violation to impede traffic. You are a scientist, so you look at the gas tank and determine it has a 20 gallon capacity. The car is exactly like yours, and you know you have been getting 15 miles per gallon. The speed limit is

60 miles per hour, and almost everyone drives at this rate, so your car has been consuming 4 gallons per hour. Using this data you estimate then that he must have driven 5 hours since his last stop.

You get into your car, and pretty soon encounter the driver trudging down the road. Anxious to demonstrate to your partner the validity of your assumptions and the wisdom of your scientific analysis, you stop, roll down your window, and ask the disgruntled and footsore hiker how long he had been driving before running out of gas. "Thirty minutes," he angrily shouts back. "Next time I'm going to fill up the gas tank when I stop, not only put in 3 gallons — and I will check the gas lines for leaks." You turn your embarrassed countenance toward your partner, who is chuckling over your error, and admit you made a mistake — not in calculations but in assumptions. Yes, your assumptions — which seemed so valid and factual when you made them — were wrong.

The theory of evolution is based on many assumptions. First and foremost is the assumption that there was no special creation. It is also based in part on the assumption of uniformitarianism, unchanging rates. But allow me to make another assumption — the assumption that God created the world and all its inhabitants in 6 days. And now let us imagine that Adam was a scientist interested in determining the age of the earth. He starts his research on the 8th day after creation, in and around the garden of Eden. He looks at himself and Eve, and realizing that they are both mature individuals, states that they and the earth are at least 20 years old. He cuts down a tree in order to build a fire, and counts the growth rings. According to this, the earth is at least 139 years old. He and Eve stroll down to the river banks, where he notices the deep channel cut by the stream. By carefully measuring the erosion rate, he estimates and concludes that 5,000 years have gone by since the stream started as a tiny trickle. They pause and marvel at the magnificent mountains in the distance, watching the sun as it slowly sinks beneath the peaks. He knows that internal pressures within the earth are slowly pushing these mountains higher—and using the present established rate, he calculates that the mountain range is at least 1.5 billion years old. The next day they explore a canyon started 750,000 years ago by a river, and marvel at the layers of rock, some formed almost 3 billion years in the past, according to his geological time scale which is based upon rock formation phenomena. He sees fossils imbedded in some of the rock—and wonders what conditions on this earth were like 1 billion years ago when this was the only form of life which was present. They stumble upon a cave, and find bones which a carbon check shows are 10,000 years old. He taps a rock with his hammer until it breaks, and finds therein a mixture of uranium and lead. A quick radiological test and he knows that at least 1 billion years have elapsed since this rock was formed. . . . And so Adam, the scientist, determines the age of the world upon which he is living—a world which according to his reasoning, observations, calculations, and assumptions is at least 3 billion years old—yet it is a world which was created just 8 days earlier.

"Absurd," you say; "you are prejudiced and biased. It is foolish to believe anything like that. Why should God create a world in that condition?" Is it? Not everything I said may be true—and much of it, such as the fossils in rocks and bones in the cave may appear unreasonable—but I defy anyone to prove that any part of my assumptions is wrong. It may not be reasonable according to our senses, but it certainly can be true. It is just as valid to make that assumption as it is to assume that the earth was formed in a "big bang" and that all life evolved from a chance encounter between the right atoms.

The only way that this assumption can be disproved is

for science to prove their theory without a doubt, and this will never be done. It would take an eyewitness account to prove that the creation theory is wrong—and yet strange as it may seem all written history indicates otherwise. The material evidence which we do have to work with can be shaped and interpreted to prove almost any theory you would care to advance. This fact is quite evident when we see the number of theories which do exist.

As an example, consider current theories concerning the origin of the universe. One group vigorously upholds Lemaitre's Big Bang idea, while the other group vehemently claims this is wrong and adheres to the Steady State Universe of Hoyle and his colleagues. Allan Broms, a scientist, in his book *Our Emerging Universe,* comments on the latter and says:

> He does not tell us how new matter comes into being, but asks us (at least for the time being) to take its gradual creation on faith (scientific faith, that is), which of course means that we will take it all back the instant any positive fact gives us the slightest excuse. Furthermore, he does not explain why this accumulation of new matter should push the older matter more and more apart to give us the expanding Universe, but again asks for another bit of scientific faith, subject to the same proviso. And when we look dubious over taking so much on faith, he properly reminds us that we ourselves have no way of explaining how matter otherwise came to be (even originally, suddenly, and in a lump), and that we are taking the Big Bang itself very nearly on faith.

And we say it takes too much faith to accept Genesis 1 literally?

The same can be said about the origin of life. Here you

must accept the philosophy of uniformitarianism. Physical processes both on earth and in the earth are thought to be subject to unchanging natural laws, and therefore more or less continuous and uniform over the past—hence the word "uniformitarianism." Once the assumption is accepted, one can study actual processes and extrapolate these into the geological past to interpret our factual findings, forming them into a genetical, historical picture. The implications of uniformitarianism in the search for the origin of life on earth are clear. You look for natural causes of the same character as are in operation at the present time. You do not—and cannot—envision some sudden event which caused life to appear all at once as a full-fledged phenomenon in every corner of the earth. Rather, the origin of life will have covered an enormous time span if measured against human standards. During this period development will have been slow, almost beyond imagination.

How firm is this theory—this assumption? Allow me to quote from a book written by M. G. Rutten, a professor of geology, entitled *The Geological Aspects of the Origin of Life on Earth,* a book published in 1962. He writes:

> So on the one hand we geologists have the possibility of studying the evolution of life on earth, of paleontological research, with a wealth of factual data. Although the gaps in the paleontological records are so large that anyone with a bias can still make a case against natural evolution, the development of paleontological research clearly points towards its general acceptance. Many gaps in the records have been lately filled by lucky finds, and we feel sure what this research is leading up to.
>
> On the other hand, there is the problem of the origin of life on earth. Here the data are extremely poor. The time elapsed is so enormous that it is diffi-

cult to prove anything at all, because the record is not only incomplete in the extreme, but also often changed beyond recognition by younger events. Moreover, such research implies a doubt toward popular views on creation and thereby provokes criticism on immaterial grounds from the side of church people: criticism which cannot be effectively answered owing to lack of data.

And we are at times ashamed and apologetic of our faith in Genesis 1?

Neither are historical dates firmly established. C. W. Ceram, in his book *Gods, Graves, and Scholars,* writes this:

How far the scholars of the West have departed from Manetho's chronology is shown by the following array of dates assigned, through the years, by different authorities to the unification of Egypt by King Menes, an event that marked the real beginning of Egyptian history and may be taken as the earliest happenings of dynastic significance: Champollian, 5867 B. C.; Lesueur, 5770; Bokh, 5702; Unger, 5613; Mariette, 5004; Brugsch, 4455; Lauth, 4157; Chabes, 4000; Lepsius, 3892; Bunsen, 3623; Eduard Meyer, 3180; Wilkinson, 2320; Palmer, 2224. Recently the date has been pushed back again, Breasted dates Menes at 3400, Georg Steindorff at 3200, and the newest research at 2900. It is significant that all dates become more difficult to determine the farther back one goes into history.

And we struggle to find a means whereby we can logically change the meaning of the word "day" in Genesis 1?

I could go on for hours citing similar examples — how Hooton in his book *Up from the Ape* devotes an entire section to explaining the tremendous significance of the Piltdown Man — a fossil we now know to have been a fraud — how White in *The Warfare of Science with Religion* flagrantly misinterprets the significance of the Chaldean cuneiforms, using them to prove the Bible is a myth, when actually they substantiate the Bible. But I feel I have shown you enough to make you realize that the scientific theory of the origin of the universe and the life it holds has not been proved — and furthermore will never be proved on this earth. It is a theory which must be accepted on faith — faith in science and its method.

But why, do you ask, is this theory so readily accepted, while religious faith is scoffed at? The answer lies in the dominant role played by science in our lives today, and in the philosophy which is accepted and adhered to by most people. The philosophy is that originated by David Hume and is called positivism. This doctrine claims that the only knowledge that has any accessible validity is the knowledge obtained by the positive — or empirical and experimental — sciences. It asserts that science gives us this positive knowledge — and denies that we can have any other knowledge but this. Reason, not faith, is the key word. Therefore religious beliefs are automatically false, since we cannot conduct a controlled experiment to prove them. To many, science is the only knowledge — serving in addition as a philosophy and religion. It can provide the answer to the common demand of our times — "Show Me."

So today to question science is almost the equivalent of being labeled a heretic. Question their theories, and your beliefs are ridiculed — your faith in other forms of knowledge made to appear groundless and foolish. In some circles to be unscientific is to be automatically wrong. The church, subjected to an almost overwhelming intellectual pressure, starts to look for methods of obtaining relief. The first avenue explored is that of modifying doctrine and interpretation to make it more reasonable — to appeal to reason, to agree with science and its theories.

Where do we start to modify? At what appears to be our most vulnerable point, of course, the doctrine of creation. After all, what difference does it make if I believe the earth is 4 billion years old? Isn't evolution also a form of creation, evidence of the power and wisdom of Almighty God? Since evolved man is constantly improving, he could never have been perfect and sinless, therefore Genesis 3 becomes a poetical way of explaining why things aren't perfect today. . . . The flood? Well, you know how events magnify when told and retold. After all, Moses had to rely on stories handed down from generation to generation. In the process a small local inundation becomes a worldwide flood. Reason tells us there just isn't enough water to cover the entire earth. . . . God leading the children of Israel in a pillar of cloud and fire? What reasonable explanation can be found for this? Well, the Israelites, in their fear, wanted to believe God was near, so they imagined this, and the writings of Moses reflect the people's imagination and impression. Actually, the smoke and fire came from a distant volcano — they just thought it was leading them, and God was using a natural phenomenon to help them. . . . The waters of the River Jordan parted? Now this could have happened if, for instance, a large rock slide upstream had temporarily held back the waters. True, God caused the avalanche, but Joshua got carried away in his description. He omitted the real facts.

And so we make the Bible reasonable — changing our interpretation to what we feel is acceptable to the public — using as our excuse the fact that none of these changes are affecting beliefs necessary to salvation. We never give to God the almighty power so rightly His — the power to suspend the forces of nature which He created — because we feel our people will never accept this. *But where do we stop?* Are the doctrines of the Trinity—the Virgin Birth—the dual nature of Christ—the Resurrection—the Ascension—salvation by grace through faith—are these doctrines reasonable? How do you tell someone to have faith in these doctrines, when you have trained him to use his reason throughout the rest of the Bible? How do you explain to him that in one case we accept the literal translation and in the next we modify? Would it not appear to the outsider that the church is itself unsure of what to believe?

The argument is often advanced that we must "stay with the times"—we must revise our teachings if we are to appeal to modern man. There is a tendency to react to this philosophy in a manner symptomatic of our times, we try to make it easy for a potential member to join, or our members to believe, asking little of them by way of mental effort. We try to make everything reasonable—instead of appealing to their faith—instead of taking the time and effort to go through a thorough explanation. We are afraid we might turn away a prospect by unreasonable demands—so every effort is made to make the instructions "easy to swallow."

In the process we try to bring God down to man, rather than taking man up to God; we try to give him a God whose action and power can be understood. We feel we are helping —and yet are we not actually depriving? For I want a God whose wisdom, power, attributes, and might are so great that my frail human mind cannot begin to understand Him. I want a God who fills me with such wonder and awe that I feel compelled to fall on my face and worship Him. I want a God so all-knowing and powerful that He can reverse the forces of nature, if necessary, to protect me. I want a God so loving that He will forgive me again and again and again.

To have this kind of God I must have faith—a faith which He gives me, using as His instruments the pastors, teachers, and members of His church. Are we doing all we can to aid in i.istilling this faith in our people today? Faith, not works, was the battle cry of the Reformation. Faith, not reason, should be the watchword of tomorrow. Thank God our church has adhered to a sound, fundamental, and conservative doctrine in the past, a doctrine based on faith. Pray God that we may continue to do so in the future.

A question you may rightly ask concerns personal application. Does all this mean that we should ignore reason in our instructions? Should we, for instance, forbid the teaching of the evolution theory in a parochial school system? No — for reason is the tool of science and philosophy, one our children will certainly be called upon to use as they continue their education. Evolution, for instance, should not only be mentioned; it should be taught as a required subject, in my way of thinking. Unless we do this, the student will feel we are trying to suppress the truth and will be all the more prone to accept the theory for fact in advanced education courses. But when it is taught, include all the "ifs" and the "buts" — and the "whys" and "therefores." If the textbook you use makes theory sound like fact — and almost all elementary texts will — then supplement your reading with others more truthful. In fact, I think there is a crying need today for a small handbook which briefly explains the weaknesses in the evolutionary theory in layman's language.

Reason or faith — which should be emphasized? Reason — which tells us that there must be a Supreme Being who established the order in nature, who wound the clock which runs the universe, and who now sits back and watches it run without interference — or faith, which tells us we have an all-powerful God who not only created the world and its inhabitants but who still today guides, controls, and directs it? Reason, which tells us that man evolved from lower mammals and is better in all respects today than he ever was in the past — or faith, which tells us that man was created by God in His image, righteous, in perfect communion with God, that man chose to sin and today pays the penalty, that man from the moment of conception is in need of a Savior? Reason, which gives to God a human form and then tells us that He could not possibly be at all places in the same instant—or faith, which tells us that He is omnipresent, always close to us, always guarding, guiding, and protecting? Reason, which tells us that God sits back and watches the world, indifferent to our individual problems—or faith, which tells us our God is omniscient, knows our thoughts, our troubles, our joys, ever stands by to help us, no matter how deserted we may feel? Reason, which tells us that God must be a stern judge constantly condemning us for breaking impossible laws—or faith, which leads us to know God as a kind and loving Father, who cherishes us as His children, who sacrificed His Son that we might live, who forgives us when we sin, who loves us with a love incomprehensible to human understanding?

What will be the predominate theme in days to come— faith in man's ability, in his reason—or faith in the almighty power of a God who has revealed Himself to us? Choose reason if you want to be in tune with the times, if you want to impress the scientific community, if you want to have popular appeal. But choose faith if you are concerned about the eternal welfare of the listener's soul. Choose faith if you want to give him that peace which reason cannot understand.

I have, in this brief treatise, attempted to show that science depends on reason, religion on faith—that science is forced, by its method, to adopt a theory such as evolution, and that this theory has many serious weaknesses. My examples of these have been few—I ask you to accept my word that there are others. I would like to share with you, however, my beliefs after a lengthy study of scientific and religious books. I believe that God created this world and its inhabitants in a period of 6 days. I believe that God created man in His image, and that my desire to sin is a result of the fall of one man, a man named Adam. I believe that the miracles of the Bible occurred as described, that God used His power to suspend the forces of nature which He once set into being. I believe that I am a child of God—not because of my works, but because Christ has atoned for my sins—an atonement which the Holy Spirit has led me to accept. I believe that I can go through life confident in the knowledge that God is in control, allowing only those things to happen which will ultimately be for my good: I believe that this faith will be challenged severely in the years in which apparent proofs will arise to support existing theories. But I believe that God will keep that faith ever present in me, and that someday that faith will be justified—the day when the cloudy lid shall be removed from my eyes and I shall know all things, the day when I stand before my Father, my God, my King, in heaven.

Prejudiced? Perhaps. Biased? Yes, I guess I am. A fool? If this means believing that very apparent physical evidence can be misinterpreted, then the accusation may be just. You, too, may be the recipient of such titles. If such should happen, and if as a result you feel insecure, then why not turn to St. Paul's first letter to the Corinthians, in the first chapter, where his inspired words tell us: "For the word of the cross is folly to those who are perishing, but to us who are being saved it is the power of God. For it is written, 'I will destroy the wisdom of the wise, and the cleverness of the clever I will thwart.' Where is the wise man? Where is the scribe? Has not God made foolish the wisdom of the world? . . . For the foolishness of God is wiser than men, and the weakness of God is stronger than men."

There was evening, and there was morning. . . . And if the story told is true, the world came boldly into view. . . . Faith—or reason? Which will it be? As you go about in your respective occupations I would like to have you take seven

159

words with you — words I have repeated so often in the past — words which I hope you will learn to use in the future. The words, in the form of a prayer, are these — *Lord, I believe; help Thou my unbelief.*

Critique
of Evolution Theory

Walter E. Lammerts, Ph. D.

Introduction

By evolution we will mean the generalized theory which holds that all kinds of plants and animals have descended from one or at best a few simple forms of one-celled organisms. Actually there are at present no *simple* creatures, since "simple" forms such as bacteria, amoeba, diatoms, and foraminifera, although one-celled, are nevertheless really very complex creatures.

Variability is often confused with evolution. Races of mankind, the many breeds of cattle, breeds of dogs, and varieties of roses are all examples of variation. Within these basic types no two individuals are exactly alike. The potential for variability is far greater in some species than in others. Roses are highly variable; but the purslane weed, *Portulaca oleracea,* is remarkably constant, even though very widespread.

In addition to having a characteristic variability potential, plants and animals occasionally mutate. Such mutations, often called "sports," occur in roses and often result in valuable varieties. Better Times, still the most widely planted sport variety, was a sport of Briarcliff. Usually these mutations are hereditary. In recent years it has been shown that they are "mistakes" in the transmission of genetic factors by the intricate DNA system. The great majority of such mistakes lead to defects, but very occasionally some are advantageous under new or unusual environmental conditions.

We might profitably consider Darwin's concept of evolution by natural selection. First of all, he considered variation as essentially unlimited, with those individuals most fitted to the environment being naturally selected. Second, he believed that in the following generation the same *range* of variability would occur. Thus in his classical discussion of the presumed origin or evolution of the giraffe he wrote:

> So under nature with the nascent giraffe, the individuals which were the highest browsers, and were able during dearths to reach even an inch or two above the others, will often have been preserved; for they will have roamed over the whole country in search of food. That the individuals of the same species often differ slightly in the relative lengths of all their parts may be seen in many works of natural history, in which careful measurements are given. These slight proportional differences, due to the laws of growth and variation, are not of the slightest use or importance to most species. But it will have been otherwise with the nascent giraffe, considering its probable habits of life; for those individuals which had some one part or several parts of their bodies rather more elongated than usual, would generally have survived. These will have intercrossed and left offspring, either inheriting the same bodily peculiarities, or with a tendency to vary again in the same manner; whilst the individuals, less favored in the

same respects, will have been the most liable to perish.

We here see that there is no need to separate single pairs, as man does, when he methodically improves a breed. Natural selection will preserve and thus separate all the superior individuals, allowing them freely to intercross, and will destroy all the inferior individuals. By this process, long continued, which exactly corresponds with what I have called unconscious selection by man, combined no doubt in a most important manner with the inherited effects of the increased use of parts [the longer neck], it seems to me almost certain that an ordinary hoofed quadruped might be converted into a giraffe.[1]

Now, as noted above, Darwin assumed (1) continuous variation, i. e., that each generation will show the same range of variation in *neck* length; and (2) the effects of use and disuse; i. e., the more the neck is stretched, the longer it gets. Darwin was driven finally to devise a scheme of pangenesis, now disproven, to explain the presumed inheritance of the effects of use or disuse.

However, Weisman in 1892, as well as later, clearly showed that the reproductive cells, instead of being developed by gemmules assembled from various parts of the body, as Darwin thought, form a continuous line from generation to generation. Various recent works show that deoxyribonucleic acid molecules (DNA), arranged in helical fashion, actually form an information code. By this means the organism develops according to a master template, or pattern. Such new information makes even clearer why the results of environment cannot be inherited.

What Are Actual Principles of Inheritance?

The Austrian monk Gregor Mendel performed a lengthy series of experiments involving the crossing of garden peas.

As a result he found that a definite statistical pattern governed the inheritance of the various characters he studied, for one example, tall vs. dwarf. The operation can be clarified by using the usual checkerboard diagram.

To begin with we have, crossing a tall with a dwarf plant

Parental (P) generation —   T T   x   t t
                              (tall, pure line)   (dwarf, pure line)

                          This crossing gives rise to

First filial (F_1) generation —   all T t

The result is that all plants in this generation are tall. Since the dwarf characteristic is recessive to the tall, it remains latent. One T factor is evidently able to make the plant grow successfully as well as two. Crossing two F_1 plants gives rise to the following results:

Gametes from Pollen

		T (50%)	t (50%)
	T (50%)	T T (50×50=25%) breed true tall	T t (50×50=25%) hybrid tall
Gametes from egg cells (ovule)	t (50%)	T t (50×50=25%) hybrid tall	t t (50×50=25%) breed true for dwarf

The second filial generation, or F_2, has a ratio of three tall to one dwarf garden pea. One third of the tall plants are TT and breed true for tall. One fourth of the F_2 will be dwarf and breed true for this recessive trait.

If two factors are involved, then $1/16$ of the F_2 generation ($1/4 \times 1/4$) will show the recessive trait. If 3 factors are involved, then ($1/4 \times 1/4 \times 1/4$) or $1/64$ will be recessive in the F_2 generation.

Later work has shown that these *major* factors may have modifying factors. So by further selection, slightly taller plants may be obtained. But the limits of this effect are soon reached, and from then on selection is no longer effective, since the strain has been thus made true breeding, or homozygous, for all factors affecting the height of the plants.

Variability thus is definitely *limited* instead of being unlimited as Darwin thought. Thus in breeding for long bud, in roses, the ultimate in bud length is achieved in five or six generations. In fact my new American Heritage owes its lovely bud form to its great-grandparents Sister Therese and Crimson Glory. But it has a bud that is only a little longer than Sister Therese. Again, yield in corn was phenomenally increased for five or six generations, after which progress slowed. Now corn breeders spend most of their time maintaining inbred lines which, when crossed, give superb hybrid vigor. They are also continuing to breed for increased disease resistance, local adaptation, and related problems. Contrary to what Darwin believed, the variability potential of such species is definitely limited, and limits are soon reached!

Is Evolution Possible by Mutation?

Various agencies, such as cosmic radiation and chemical mutagens, cause mutations, but there is considerable evidence that a basic percentage of mutations are spontaneous. The DNA upon duplication does not *always* give a perfect replica of itself. In some cases we know exactly what has happened. Thus in sickle-cell anemia the normal sequence of amino acids in the hemoglobin of the red blood corpuscles has had one replacement. This is sufficient to cause a defective mechanism. The chart on the following page will show what is considered to have taken place.

Now, valine is not poisonous or in itself undesirable. In fact, in its proper *location* it is one of the essential components of hemoglobin. But for some odd reason, in this *location,* replacing one of the two glutamic acid molecules, it causes a serious defect. Just how this defect occurs we do not know. Conversion of the glutamic acid to valine is one

Normal Sequence in Red Blood Cell		Sequence in Red Blood Cell in Sickle-Cell Anemia
valine		valine
histadine		histadine
leucine		leucine
threonine		threonine
proline		proline
glutamic acid	— replaced by —	valine
glutamic acid		glutamic acid
lysine		lysine

possibility, or *substitution* of a valine molecule for the glutamic acid one is another and possibly more likely. But in any case we do know that somehow in the division of the DNA chain this mistake was made.

Can these "mistakes" or chance changes in the DNA alignment of amino acids really explain the origin of species and the remarkable variation we see around us? Elliot G. Watson,[2] a British zoologist, lists four examples of life histories that simply cannot be explained by orthodox evolution theories. Thus the coral reef crab has claws so small as to be useless as weapons. But their backward curving teeth grasp the slippery bodies of small sea anemones, detaching them carefully from their hold on the rocks without injury. They are then held close to the pirate crab's mouth and continue to operate their tentacles so as to capture small creatures. These the crab, with his free front pair of walking legs, removes as dainty tidbits, leaving those he dislikes for the anemones, which are finally released unharmed.

Are these adaptations to be explained by chance mutations? Did a chance modification of claws due to a "mistake" in duplication of some DNA molecule prompt some ancestral crab to detach an anemone for the mere fun of it and by chance hold it near its mouth? If so, the crab passed on to its offspring this behavior tendency, and so through natural selection the crab species developed their close association with various anemones, the species differing, of course, to make the problem more complex, for each species of pirate crab. This, Watson says, he cannot accept—and I agree.

Are Mutations Ever Advantageous?

Under new environmental conditions mutations sometimes are advantageous. Thus bacteria catastrophically exposed to high levels of penicillin or streptomycin die. But occasionally one lives because it undergoes a mutation, giving it a tolerance for one of these antibiotics. In penicillin this is a step-by-step phenomenon giving rise to the circumstance that the increasing of dosage rates is followed by increasingly resistant strains—but always up to certain limits, of course. In the case of streptomycin, the change to maximum resistance is effected in one mutation, and from there on no further increase in tolerance is developed. This at first looks good for our evolution-minded colleagues, but Pratt and Dufrenoy,[3] bacteriologists at the University of California Medical Center, point out that these resistant types are lower in metabolic ratio and so are at a *disadvantage* under normal circumstances in cultures free of antibiotics. They are then soon "swamped out" by the normal type. Furthermore, there is no evidence that these resistant types ever achieve a metabolic or reproductive ratio that is *superior* to that of the normal type.

Mutation thus only increases variability potential, and sometimes this allows a species to survive in areas or circumstances where otherwise there would be complete annihilation. But this variability potential, even including possible mutation, is definitely limited for each species by the pattern of development. This evidently sets limits to the range. Thus, to use a somewhat facetious example, one does not have mutations causing a pair of wings to grow on the backs of human beings, but frequently an *extra pair* of wings are formed in the fruit fly, which ordinarily has only one pair.

Also, the more complex the organism, the less chance there is for mutations of advantage to occur, even under new environmental conditions. Thus my own neutron radiation experiments with roses resulted in hundreds of mutations, some of possible horticultural value. However, without exception all irradiated forms were either weaker or more sterile than the same variety without radiation.

What Natural Selection Can and Cannot Do

Miss H. T. Band in a 1965 paper on natural selection in the fruit fly *Drosophila melanogaster*,[4] has given some rather remarkable evidence that natural selection does *not* increase the frequency of the most highly viable true breeding lines, or homozygotes, in natural populations. Her population studies were made in 1961 after the unusually severe winter of 1960−61 at Amherst, Mass. The Sept. 10 and 11 temperatures were the highest on record, and samples were collected during this period. Also in 1962 collections were made during the driest season on record. The results of genetic analysis of variability and viability in 1961 and 1962 were compared with those of 1960 and some earlier ones of the period 1947−49.

Her conclusions, briefly summarized, are as follows: Natural selection is highly efficient in maintaining population fitness during changing environmental conditions. The effects, however, are manifest only in the heterozygotes. Stabilizing selection has led to the retention of most components of genetic diversity. There is no evidence of improvement among the homozygotes (those breeding true for various mutations).

Also no decrease in the magnitude of the genetic load was shown. Most load components remained concealed in the random heterozygotes. Thus the joint effects of stabilization and directional selection appear directed to the interreaction of genes and their complexes in the heterozygous condition.

The effects of selection in the more stringent environment have possibly caused changes in the genetic structure of the population, with a resultant slight reduction in total genetic diversity.

The most interesting conclusion is hardly stressed sufficiently by Band. This is that there is *no evidence* that selection has been primarily directed toward elimination of harmful mutants or that such variants have substantially reduced the viability of the heterozygote.

According to the mutation theory the only source of new distinct features leading to species formation are mutations. These must be gradually accumulated in true breeding condition, since species differ from one another in various traits that *are constant*. Yet Band's research clearly shows that even the most viable true breeding mutations, or homozygous ones, *do not increase in number* as a result of natural selection. Also no improvement in their viability occurs. Since even drastic mutational changes do not show harmful effects in the heterozygous condition, there is no mechanism for eliminating them. Now, the ratio of harmful to neutral or even possibly slightly beneficial mutations is about 1,000 to 1. So if a species evolved by mutations, the genetic load of drastic or harmful mutations would be so high in a few hundred generations as to result in almost all offspring having some defect.

The fortunate fact is that this is still not true, even in human beings (although we are approaching it). This argues for special creation of the human species unit in the not-too-distant past.

Evolution: An Overview and Examination of Evidences

1. Harold C. Bold, *Morphology of Plants* (New York: Harper & Brothers, 1957), p. 4.
2. Samuel L. Clemens, *Life on the Mississippi* (New York: Harper & Brothers, 1874), p. 156.
3. G. Ledyard Stebbins, *Processes of Organic Evolution* (Englewood Cliffs: Prentice-Hall, 1966), pp. 1 f.
4. Theodosius Dobzhansky, *Mankind Evolving* (New Haven: Yale University Press, 1962), p. 321.
5. Jean Rostand, *Can Man Be Modified?* (New York: Basic Books, 1959), p. 23.
6. Bruce Wallace, *Chromosomes, Giant Molecules, and Evolution* (New York: W. W. Norton & Co., 1966), p. 76.
7. Bruce Stewart, "On Teaching Evolution," *The American Biology Teacher*, 24 (April 1962), 272.
8. Frederick C. Steward, "Botany in the Biology Curriculum," *Bioscience*, 17 [2] (Feb. 1967), 88.
9. L. G. Becking and M. Baas, "On the Origin of Life," *The Evolution of Living Organisms*, ed. G. W. Leeper (Parkville: Melbourne University Press, 1962), pp. 38 f.
10. Richard S. Young and Cyril Ponnamperuma, "Life: Origin and Evolution," *Science*, 143 (1964), 384.
11. Edward N. Willmer, *Cytology and Evolution* (New York: Academic Press, 1960), p. 406.

12. Paul R. Ehrlich and Richard W. Holm, "Population Biology," *Science*, 139 (1963), 242; and *The Process of Evolution* (New York: McGraw-Hill, 1963), pp. 309 f.

13. Norwood Russell Hanson, "Galileo's Discoveries in Dynamics," *Science*, 147 (1965), 472 f.

14. "God, Man, and Geology," *Newsweek*, 62 (Dec. 23, 1963), 48.

15. Sigurdur Thorarinsson, *Surtsey: The New Island in the North Atlantic*, trans. Sölvi Eysteinsson (New York: Viking Press, 1967), pp. 37—41.

16. Jack L. Hough, *Geology of the Great Lakes* (Urbana: University of Illinois Press, 1958), pp. 32 f.

17. Frederick Elder, *Crisis in Eden* (Nashville: Abingdon Press, 1970), pp. 62—66.

18. Theodosius Dobzhansky, "Evolution of Genes and Genes in Evolution," *Cold Spring Harbor Symposia on Quantitative Biology*, 24 (1959), p. 22.

19. Bernhard Rensch, *Evolution Above the Species Level* (London: Methuen, 1959), p. 279.

20. David J. Merrell, *Evolution and Genetics* (New York: Holt, Rinehart & Winston, 1962), p. 95.

21. George Gaylord Simpson, "Organisms and Molecules in Evolution," *Science*, 146 (1964), 1536.

22. Ehrlich and Holm, *The Process of Evolution*, p. 66.

23. John W. Saunders Jr., "Death in Embryonic Systems," *Science*, 154 (1966), 604—611.

24. Ehrlich and Holm, *The Process of Evolution*, p. 259.

25. D. Dwight Davis, "Comparative Anatomy and the Evolution of Vertebrates," *Genetics, Paleontology, and Evolution*, ed. Glenn L. Jepsen, Ernst Mayr, and George Gaylord Simpson (Princeton: Princeton University Press, 1949), p. 73.

26. Wilbert H. Rusch Sr., "Human Fossils," Ch. 9 in *Rock Strata and the Bible Record*, ed. Paul A. Zimmerman (St. Louis: Concordia Publishing House, 1970), pp. 133—177.

27. George S. Carter, *Animal Evolution: A Study of Recent Views of Its Causes* (London: Sidgwick & Jackson, 1951), p. 180.

28. Hampton L. Carson, "Genetic Conditions Which Promote or Retard the Formation of Species," *Cold Spring Harbor Symposia on Quantitative Biology*, 24 (1959), p. 95.

29. Peter Brian Medawar, "A Biological Retrospect," *Bioscience*, 16 [2] (Feb. 1966), 94.

Analysis of So-Called Evidences of Evolution

1. Gerald A. Kerkut, *Implications of Evolution* (New York: Pergamon Press, 1960), p. 157.
2. William H. George, *The Scientist in Action: A Scientific Study of His Methods* (New York: Emerson Books, 1938), p. 321.
3. James B. Conant, *Science and Common Sense* (New Haven: Yale University Press, 1951), p. 37.
4. Louis Bounoure, "Evolutionnisme et Progres Humain," *Le Monde et la Vie,* Oct. 1963, pp. 53 – 56.
5. Louis Bounoure, "Le Evolutionnisme," *Le Monde et la Vie,* March 1964, pp. 55 – 56.
6. Charles Darwin, *Origin of Species,* Everyman's Library Ed. (New York: E. P. Dutton & Co., 1956), p. xxii.
7. Ernst Mayr, "Evolution vs. Special Creation," *American Biology Teacher,* Vol. 33, No. 1, p. 49.
8. Solly Zuckermann, *Functional Affinities of Man, Monkeys, and Apes* (New York: Harcourt, Brace & Co., 1933), p. 155.
9. Anna M. MacLeod and Leslie S. Cobley, eds., *Contemporary Botanical Thought* (Chicago: Quadrangle Books, 1962), p. 97.
10. *News-Sentinel,* Fort Wayne, Ind., Tuesday, July 11, 1950, editorial page.
11. *Smithsonian Treasury of Science,* II, 517.
12. Austin H. Clark, *Zoogenesis* (Baltimore: The Williams & Wilkins Co., 1930), pp. 235 – 36.
13. E. P. Stibbe, *Journal of Anatomy,* 72 (1927 – 28), 159 – 72.
14. L. Vialleton, *L'origine des etres vivants,* p. 164.
15. John Cameron, *Transactions of the Royal Society of Canada,* 12 (1918), 179.
16. G. R. De Beer and W. E. Swinton, in chapter in *Studies in Fossil Vertebrates,* ed. T. S. Wastall (London: The Athlone Press, 1958).
17. Alfred F. Huettner, *Fundamentals of Comparative Embryology of the Vertebrates* (New York: Macmillan Co., 1943), p. 48.
18. *The Toledo Blade,* Sept. 30, 1965, reported by Ray Bruner, science editor.
19. "Organic Compounds in Carbonaceous Chondrites," *Science,* Sept. 24, 1965, pp. 1455 ff.
20. William W. Rubey, *Annals of N. Y. Academy of Sciences,* 69 (Sept. 30, 1957), 255 – 376.

21. Mlle. S. Leclercq, "Evidence of Vascular Plants in the Cambrian," *Evolution,* 10 (June 1956), 109–13.

22. Daniel I. Axelrod, "Evolution of the Psilophytales," *Evolution,* 13 (June 1959), 264.

23. See Wilbert H. Rusch, "The Revelation of Palynology," *Creation Research Society Quarterly,* 5, 3 (Dec. 1968), 103–105.

24. Arnold Lunn, *The Revolt Against Reason* (London: Eyre & Spottiswoode, 1950), p. 134.

25. Glenn L. Jepsen, Ernst Mayr, and George G. Simpson, eds., *Genetics, Paleontology, and Evolution* (Princeton: Princeton University Press, 1949), p. 74.

26. Ernst Mayr, *Animal Species and Evolution* (Cambridge: Belknap Press, 1963), pp. 163, 287, 168.

27. Theodosius Dobzhansky, *Mankind Evolving* (New Haven: Yale University Press, 1962), p. 171.

28. R. J. Mason, "The Sterkfontein Stone Artifacts and Their Makers," *South African Archaeological Bulletin,* No. 17 (1962), p. 109. J. T. Robinson, "Sterkfontein Stratigraphy and the Significance of the Extension Site," *South African Archaeological Bulletin,* No. 17 (1962), p. 87.

29. For a more detailed discussion see Wilbert H. Rusch Sr., "Human Fossils," ch. 9, *Rock Strata and the Bible Record,* ed. Paul A. Zimmerman (St. Louis: Concordia Publishing House, 1970), pp. 133 to 177.

30. Jean Piveteau, *Origine de l'homme* (Paris: Librairie Hachette, 1962), p. 99.

The Word of God Today

1. *Handbook of The Lutheran Church—Missouri Synod,* 1969, p. 15.

2. Theodore G. Tappert, ed., *The Book of Concord: The Confessions of the Evangelical Lutheran Church* (Philadelphia: Fortress Press, 1959), pp. 503–505.

3. *Christianity Today,* X, 5 (Dec. 3, 1965), 243.

4. *Proceedings of the Forty-Sixth Regular Convention of The Lutheran Church—Missouri Synod,* Detroit, Mich., June 16–25, 1965, p. 292. Hereafter called Detroit Proceedings.

5. Ibid., Resolution 2-31, p. 102.

6. John Warwick Montgomery, "Lutheran Hermeneutics and Hermeneutics Today," in *Aspects of Biblical Hermeneutics, Concordia Theological Monthly Occasional Papers No. 1* (1966), p. 86, n. 37.

7. Sören Kierkegaard, *Concluding Unscientific Postscript,* quoted in Gordon H. Clark, *Revealed Religion* (1965), p. 9.

8. Rudolf Bultmann, *The Study of the Synoptic Gospels,* trans. Frederick C. Grant, in *Form Criticism* (New York: Harper Torch Books, 1962), p. 61.

9. Hans Werner Bartsch, ed., *Kerygma and Myth: A Theological Debate* (1960), p. 144.

10. *Theologische Zeitschrift,* XIII (1957), pp. 409 – 417.

11. James M. Robinson and John B. Cobb Jr., eds., *The New Hermeneutic,* Vol. II in *New Frontiers in Theology* (New York: Harper & Row, 1964), p. 51.

12. Donald T. Rowlingson, "The Gospel Perspective and the Quest of the Historical Jesus," *Journal of Bible and Religion* (Boston University School of Theology) XXXIII, 4 (October 1965), 331 – 32.

13. Robert Boling, *Journal of Bible and Religion,* Vol. XXXIII, No. 2 (April 1965), p. 166.

14. "What Some Scientists Say About God and the Supernatural," *Christianity Today,* IX, 23 (Aug. 27, 1965), 1156.

15. "Organic Compounds in Carbonaceous Chondrite," *Science* (Sept. 24, 1965), p. 1455 ff.

16. Edwin C. Webb and Malcolm Dixon, *Enzymes* (New York: Academic Press, Inc., 1964), p. 669.

17. Peter T. Mora, "The Folly of Probability," in *The Origins of Prebiological Systems and of the Molecular Martrices,* ed. Sidney W. Fox (New York: Academic Press, 1965), p. 45.

18. Robert Preus, "Notes on the Inerrancy of Scripture," *Concordia Theological Monthly,* June 1967, pp. 366 – 67.

19. Edward Young, in *Westminster Theological Journal,* May 1963, p. 169.

20. W. M. Oesch, "Die Lehre von der Inspiration und ihre Anwendung auf die Urgeschichte," *Lutherischer Rundblick,* 8:2 (May 1960), 74 – 75.

21. *Interpreter's Bible* (New York: Abingdon Cokesbury Press, 1952), I, 471.

22. Bernard Ramm, *The Christian View of Science and Scripture* (Grand Rapids: William B. Eerdmans, 1954), p. 38.

23. Harry Emerson Fosdick, *The Modern Use of the Bible* (New York: Association Press, 1924), pp. 46 ff.

24. Carl Gaenssle, "A Look at Current Biblical Cosmologies," *Concordia Theological Monthly*, XXIII, 10 (October 1952), 743.

25. Frederick A. Filby, *Creation Revealed* (Pickering & Inglis, 1965), p. 72.

26. Robert D. Preus, "Different Modern Approaches to the Creation Account of Genesis 1-2," pp. 1—2.

27. Herbert Carl Leupold, *Exposition of Genesis* (The Wartburg Press, 1942), p. 25.

28. Preus, "Different Modern Approaches," p. 8.

29. *Scripta Hierosolymitana*, Vol. 8, Studies in the Bible, ed. Chaim Robin (Jerusalem: Magnes Press, Hebrew University), p. 95.

30. The Anchor Bible, *Genesis* (Garden City, N. Y.: Doubleday and Co., 1964), pp. 8—9.

31. Edward J. Young, *Westminster Theological Journal*, XXV, 1 (November 1962), 15.

32. Young, ibid., p. 5.

33. P. G. Fothergill, *Evolution and Christians* (London: Longmans, 1961), p. 327.

34. Alexander Heidel, *The Gilgamesh Epic and Old Testament Parallels* (Chicago: University of Chicago Press, 1949), pp. 142—43.

35. Helmut Thielicke, *How the World Began* (Philadelphia: Muhlenberg Press, 1961), pp. 175—76.

36. Gerhard von Rad, *Genesis* (Philadelphia: Westminster Press, 1961), pp. 92—93.

37. R. C. H. Lenski, *The Interpretation of St. Paul's Epistles to the Colossians, to the Thessalonians, to Timothy, to Titus, and to Philemon* (Columbus: Lutheran Book Concern, 1937), p. 575.

38. William F. Arndt and F. Wilbur Gingrich, *A Greek-English Lexicon of the New Testament* (University of Chicago Press, 1957), pp. 732—33.

39. Walter R. Roehrs, "The Creation Account of Genesis," *Concordia Theological Monthly*, XXXVI (May 1965), 317—18.

40. George Gaylord Simpson, *This View of Life* (New York: Harcourt Brace & Co., 1964), p. 232.

41. Curtly F. Mather, in *Science Ponders Religion,* ed. Harlow Shapley (New York: Appleton-Century-Crofts, Inc., 1960), pp. 37—38.

42. *Time,* Aug. 1, 1960, p. 45.

44. Robert D. Preus,
    Confessional Ap
    Strata and the E
    Concordia Pub!

45. Preus, "Guidir

46. Joseph Cambe
    1959), pp. 38

47. E. O. James,
    F. A. Praeg

48. Alexander Heidel, ...
    Press, 1942), pp. 103–105.

49. B. Malinowski, *Magic, Science, and Religion* (Doubleday Anchor
    Book, 1954), p. 100.

50. B. S. Childs, *Myth and Reality in the Old Testament* (London:
    SCM Press, 1962), p. 42.

51. Quoted in Gerhard von Rad, *Genesis, A Commentary* (Phil-
    adelphia: Westminster Press, 1961), p. 98.

Critique of Evolution Theory

1. Charles Darwin, *The Origin of Species* (Modern Library, Random
   House, Inc.), p. 161.

2. Elliot G. Watson, "Hidden Heart of Nature," *Saturday Evening
   Post*, 284 (May 27, 1961), 32–33.

3. Robertson Pratt and Jean Dufrenoy, *Antibiotics*, 2d. ed. (Philadelphia: Lippincott, 1953), p. 343.

4. H. T. Band, "Natural Selection and Concealed Genetic Variability
   in a Natural Population of *D. melanogaster*," *Evolution*, 18:3
   (1965), 334–404.

44. Robert D. Preus, "Guiding Theological Principles: A Lutheran Confessional Approach to the Doctrine of Creation," in *Rock Strata and the Bible Record,* ed. Paul A. Zimmerman (St. Louis: Concordia Publishing House, 1970), p. 19.

45. Preus, "Guiding Principles," p. 21.

46. Joseph Cambell, *The Masks of God* (New York: Viking Press, 1959), pp. 387–88.

47. E. O. James, *Myth and Ritual in the Ancient Near East* (New York: F. A. Praeger, 1958), pp. 202–203.

48. Alexander Heidel, *The Babylonian Genesis* (University of Chicago Press, 1942), pp. 103–105.

49. B. Malinowski, *Magic, Science, and Religion* (Doubleday Anchor Book, 1954), p. 100.

50. B. S. Childs, *Myth and Reality in the Old Testament* (London: SCM Press, 1962), p. 42.

51. Quoted in Gerhard von Rad, *Genesis, A Commentary* (Philadelphia: Westminster Press, 1961), p. 98.

Critique of Evolution Theory

1. Charles Darwin, *The Origin of Species* (Modern Library, Random House, Inc.), p. 161.

2. Elliot G. Watson, "Hidden Heart of Nature," *Saturday Evening Post,* 284 (May 27, 1961), 32–33.

3. Robertson Pratt and Jean Dufrenoy, *Antibiotics,* 2d. ed. (Philadelphia: Lippincott, 1953), p. 343.

4. H. T. Band, "Natural Selection and Concealed Genetic Variability in a Natural Population of *D. melanogaster,*" *Evolution,* 18:3 (1965), 334–404.

23. Harry Emerson Fosdick, *The Modern Use of the Bible* (New York: Association Press, 1924), pp. 46 ff.

24. Carl Gaenssle, "A Look at Current Biblical Cosmologies," *Concordia Theological Monthly*, XXIII, 10 (October 1952), 743.

25. Frederick A. Filby, *Creation Revealed* (Pickering & Inglis, 1965), p. 72.

26. Robert D. Preus, "Different Modern Approaches to the Creation Account of Genesis 1-2," pp. 1 – 2.

27. Herbert Carl Leupold, *Exposition of Genesis* (The Wartburg Press, 1942), p. 25.

28. Preus, "Different Modern Approaches," p. 8.

29. *Scripta Hierosolymitana*, Vol. 8, Studies in the Bible, ed. Chaim Robin (Jerusalem: Magnes Press, Hebrew University), p. 95.

30. The Anchor Bible, *Genesis* (Garden City, N. Y.: Doubleday and Co., 1964), pp. 8 – 9.

31. Edward J. Young, *Westminster Theological Journal*, XXV, 1 (November 1962), 15.

32. Young, ibid., p. 5.

33. P. G. Fothergill, *Evolution and Christians* (London: Longmans, 1961), p. 327.

34. Alexander Heidel, *The Gilgamesh Epic and Old Testament Parallels* (Chicago: University of Chicago Press, 1949), pp. 142 – 43.

35. Helmut Thielicke, *How the World Began* (Philadelphia: Muhlenberg Press, 1961), pp. 175 – 76.

36. Gerhard von Rad, *Genesis* (Philadelphia: Westminster Press, 1961), pp. 92 – 93.

37. R. C. H. Lenski, *The Interpretation of St. Paul's Epistles to the Colossians, to the Thessalonians, to Timothy, to Titus, and to Philemon* (Columbus: Lutheran Book Concern, 1937), p. 575.

38. William F. Arndt and F. Wilbur Gingrich, *A Greek-English Lexicon of the New Testament* (University of Chicago Press, 1957), pp. 732 – 33.

39. Walter R. Roehrs, "The Creation Account of Genesis," *Concordia Theological Monthly*, XXXVI (May 1965), 317 – 18.

40. George Gaylord Simpson, *This View of Life* (New York: Harcourt Brace & Co., 1964), p. 232.

41. Curtly F. Mather, in *Science Ponders Religion*, ed. Harlow Shapley (New York: Appleton-Century-Crofts, Inc., 1960), pp. 37 – 38.

42. *Time*, Aug. 1, 1960, p. 45.